Teaching Children with
Learning Difficulties

Teaching Children with Learning Difficulties

Ron Gulliford

NFER-NELSON

Published by The NFER-NELSON Publishing Company Ltd.,
Darville House, 2 Oxford Road East,
Windsor, Berkshire SL4 1DF

and in the United States of America by

NFER-NELSON, 242 Cherry Street, Philadelphia, PA 19106–1906.
Tel: (215) 238 0939. Telex: 244489.

First Published 1985
Reprinted 1986, 1987
© 1985 Ron Gulliford

Library of Congress Cataloging in Publication data

Gulliford, R.
  Teaching children with learning difficulties.

  1. Learning disabled children—Education—Great Britain.   I. Title.
LC4706.G7G85   1985   371.9′0941   85–15352
ISBN 0-7005-0551-2

Printed in Great Britain by A. Wheaton & Co. Ltd, Exeter

ISBN 0 7005 0551 2
Code 8142 02 1

Contents

Foreword

The intention of this book is to provide teachers in initial training, and others who are interested, with an account of recent changes in ideas about the needs of children and young people with learning difficulties and with an introduction to their education.

At the heart of change is the view that children with difficulty in learning have the same needs as others for the learning and personal development which schools provide through the curriculum and through full participation in the school community. How to translate that view into practice is not a question for which there are simple answers. It requires continued experiment, the evaluation of experience, the provision of resources and especially the essential resource of concerned and informed teachers.

There is now a wide range of books and journal articles relevant to the issues considered in this book. The references in the text are intended as signposts to some of these and the suggestions for further reading indicate others.

I am grateful to Brenda Cox for typing the manuscript and to Audrey Griffiths for many kinds of help during its preparation. I would like to acknowledge my debt to colleagues and students in the Department of Special Education, University of Birmingham, and to the teachers in schools so readily sharing their experience with us.

CHAPTER 1
Difficulties in Learning

Most of us have had experience of difficulty in learning certain things. Secure in the knowledge that we learn most things well and perhaps some things very well, we are even confident enough to boast or joke about subjects or everyday skills in which we are hopelessly incompetent. Some men, invited to take part in some singing, will exclaim 'Me sing? I'm tone deaf; I only sing in my bath.' Few however would admit to being less than a good car driver.

For many children in school and for some adults, failure to learn certain things is a more serious matter. An adolescent who cannot read is unlikely to boast about it. Many adults who cannot read go to great lengths to conceal this inability – even from their family – and find ways of 'getting by' in their work and in the many affairs of daily life which require reading and writing.

At one time, the basic goal of schooling for the majority was the achievement of literacy and numeracy. This remains crucial but the extension of secondary education to all, the raising of educational standards and of the academic demands for entry into skilled employment and vocations have increased the significance of even moderate failures in learning. Young people with already formed vocational aspirations which require certain examination passes are likely to be worried by failures in essential subjects such as English or mathematics even though they are successful in others and have personal qualities and interests suited to their proposed vocation. Some have a weakness in spelling which goes well beyond the lapses and individual errors that many people display. It is or should be part of the normal process of teaching to give further help, encouragement and support to pupils who experience such difficulties, with advice and assistance where needed from specialists such as remedial teachers, educational psychologists or counsellors.

A more serious problem is presented by children and young people whose difficulty in learning the basic skills of reading, writing or mathematics is an impediment to their full participation in the curriculum of their age group. If not remedied, the disability becomes an increasing handicap as the child gets older and as schoolwork depends more on reading and writing. It is liable to result in an unsatisfying and unenjoyable experience of school; it may result in anxiety and loss of self-confidence or in giving up and opting out. Reactions to failure – as with other human predicaments – depend on many variable factors: the individual's personality, the existence of compensatory successes and interests; the degree of support given by parents and teachers; the expectations of the social environment.

The effects of failure are not limited to the obvious aspects of school achievement. Lack of independent reading skill deprives a child of access to the wealth of knowledge and language in books and the vicarious experience of human situations and emotions in stories and novels – not to mention the pleasure and enjoyment. There are of course other experiences of living, doing, conversing and of television which provide compensation but it is not so easy to compensate for limitations in written expression which is a means of extending language skills and organizing thoughts.

We do not normally think of these difficulties as disabilities comparable to physical or sensory impairments although there is some currency for the term learning disability especially in the USA. There is some justification for doing so since it is a recognition that the child may have a real learning problem and is not just lazy or unmotivated (though they may be). As with other disabilities, the individual is less likely to be blamed for their failure and more importantly it focuses attention on what can be done to reduce the handicapping effects and on what special adaptations are needed.

The frequency of learning difficulties

Difficulties in learning such basic educational skills as reading, spelling and mathematics are more frequent than is often realized and constitute a problem which requires just as well organized educational measures as are provided for able pupils. During the last 30 or so years, many surveys by local education authorities, teachers' organizations and major research projects have provided the data for these conclusions.

The first surveys in the post-war years were occasioned by national concern about illiteracy which had been revealed in recruits during the war. A survey in 1948 undertaken for the Ministry of Education estimated that the reading standards of 11-year-olds had dropped by over a year since 1938. The proportion of 15-year-olds who were illiterate (taken as reading ages below seven years) was 1.4 per cent and of semi-literates (taken as reading ages between seven and nine years) was 4.3 per cent. Further studies at intervals showed a welcome improvement: by 1964 reading levels had improved by about 17 months of reading age on average. A national survey in 1972 showed that improvement had levelled off, perhaps even declined a little. It is discussed in the Bullock Report (DES, 1975).

Other studies also indicated improvement. Hammond (1967) had surveyed reading achievement in Brighton in 1947 and did so again in 1962. While the percentage of boys aged 10 to 12 years with reading ages of less than eight years had dropped from 15.1 per cent to 10.5 per cent, the figures still indicated a hard core of backwardness in reading. This was also suggested by a study in Kent. Morris (1966) found that 14 per cent of a sample of eight-year-olds were not able to read at all or were reading extremely poorly and that half of those continued to be poor readers into their secondary schools.

Two major multi-disciplinary research studies have provided information about a range of difficulties in development and learning as well as the personal and environmental factors involved. The first of these, the National Child Development Study, followed the development and progress of 11,000 children born in one week in March 1958. At the age of seven, 10 per cent had barely made a start on learning to read; 0.4 per cent were attending special schools on account of various disabilities.

Teachers reported that 5 per cent were receiving special help in ordinary schools because of mental or educational backwardness and considered that a further 8 per cent would benefit from such help. The findings that 13 per cent of the 11,000 seven-year-olds were either receiving or deemed to need some form of special help occasioned some surprise at the time although it was consistent with other findings such as those quoted earlier (Kellmer Pringle *et al.*, 1966).

It is interesting therefore to see what the situation was when this large national sample was followed up at age 16 (Fogelman, 1976). It was found that 3 per cent of the young people had been ascertained as in need of special education and 1.9 per cent were in fact still attending special schools. Of those in ordinary schools, 7 per cent were receiving help on account of 'educational or mental backwardness' and teachers said that such help was desirable but not being given in the case of another 2 per cent. Five per cent were receiving help because of behaviour difficulties and another 3 per cent were deemed to require it. Special help in relation to physical or sensory disabilities was given for 1 per cent and a further 0.5 per cent were thought to need it. Thus at 16 years of age 20 per cent of pupils were considered to have been in need of some form of special assistance, 11 per cent requiring it because of learning difficulties.

Two other findings, reported on the basis of teachers' judgements, underline the educational problem which some young people have, even at the point of leaving school. Teachers were asked 'Can this child read well enough to cope with everyday needs (e.g. newspapers, notices etc)?' and 'Can this child do all the calculations required by an everyday shopper?' The answers to the first question were in the negative for 1.6 per cent of the sample and for the second question for 2.6 per cent.

The second major research study, the Isle of Wight study, was undertaken to discover the prevalence of intellectual and educational retardation, emotional and behaviour difficulties and physical handicaps. All children on the island aged between 9 and 12 were studied by a multi-disciplinary team (medical, educational and psychological). The prevalence of intellectual retardation (using, for the purpose of this survey, a criterion of IQ below 70 on an individual test of intelligence), was found to be 2.5 per cent. It is worth noting that nearly half of these were in ordinary schools rather than special schools, a significant factor in their placement being that they had made some progress in reading (Rutter *et al.*, 1970).

Reading backwardness was defined as reading ages for accuracy and comprehension on an individual test (the Neale Analysis of Reading) which were more than 28 months below chronological age level. This degree of backwardness was found in 8 per cent of the sample. The researchers commented that 28 months' backwardness is a severe degree of educational handicap and that there were many more children with lesser problems but great enough to constitute a marked handicap in school.

A distinction has commonly been made on the basis that some children are slow in learning to read because they are not so intelligent as others and that their poor reading is part of a general backwardness; others are brighter children who are achieving much less well than might be expected for their level of intelligence. The researchers therefore identified the percentage of children whose reading achievement was 28 months below the level predicted for their level of intelligence as well as age, that is, those who were specifically retarded in reading and not just generally backward. They found that about 4 per cent had a specific retardation in reading. Moreover, when these were followed up 28 months later, they had only made ten months' improvement in accuracy and 13 months in reading comprehension. Only one was less than two years behind his age level in reading. Later both groups were followed up when they were aged 15½. Both groups were reading at the nine-year level. Although the average IQ of the specifically retarded group was 98 and that of the reading backward group was 85, the latter were slightly better in reading (Yule, 1973).

It is worth noting that the reading ability of the children with reading backwardness and with specific reading retardation was as poor as that of the intellectually retarded group whose average IQ was 21 points below that of the reading backward group and 33 points below the specifically retarded. The three groups were also equally poor in spelling at a level 3½ years below their chronological age. Attainments in arithmetic were also generally poor but not so low as those of the intellectually retarded. It is important to realize that some intelligent pupils have specific difficulties.

How far can the findings of the Isle of Wight study be generalized to other parts of the country? The researchers expressed the cautious conclusion that because the social conditions on the Isle of Wight are generally better than those existing in the poor areas of most big cities, it is unlikely that the rate of handicap elsewhere would be less. In fact, a comparative study in a London borough using the same tests and criteria found that 19 per cent were backward in reading and 9.9 per cent were specifically retarded in reading (Rutter *et al.*, 1975). In a research beginning in 1965, Clark (1979) surveyed the reading attainment of all the seven-year-olds in Dunbartonshire. Of the 1,544 children, 15 per cent were without any independent reading skill and when retested a year later half of them were still requiring assistance.

The findings of these researches are supported by surveys which estimate the size of the problem as perceived by teachers. In Australia, Andrews *et al.* (1979) asked a sample of secondary schools how many pupils had learning difficulties, defined as 'those who display continuing difficulty in basic school learning such that they fail to respond to the usual range of teaching strategies employed by regular classroom teachers and require the support of specially trained personnel.' The main finding was that 11 per cent of pupils had learning difficulties. An inquiry about the education of slow learners in 158 secondary schools undertaken by HMIs in 1967–68 was based on questionnaires completed by the schools and also on visits to the school (DES, 1971). As the report says: 'the size of the group designated "slow learners" may cause surprise to some but tends to confirm estimates reached elsewhere.' Fourteen per cent of the total school population of the schools visited were judged to be 'slow learners'; more than one school in seven estimated that 20 per cent of its pupils needed some special help.

How special provision has developed

It may be a matter of surprise that after a century of compulsory education there should still be so many pupils who make poor progress in learning basic educational skills and that there is no consensus about how they may be best helped to benefit from their schooling. The problem however only began to be tackled more thoroughly after the Second World War. There was publicly expressed concern, partly stemming from the awareness of poor literary standards which had been revealed in recruits during the war. The 1948 survey referred to on p. 3 was partly a result of that concern. The new arrangements for handicapped pupils which followed from the 1944 Education Act also played a part in stimulating provision.

In pre-war years, special schooling was available for children who were blind, deaf, physically and mentally 'defective' (as they were then termed). In the ordinary schools, from which the majority left at 14, there was little special help other than that which might be given by sympathetic and skilful teachers. There were some special classes for the 'dull and backward'; there was the C stream class and in some areas the practice lingered on of keeping a pupil down in a lower class for a year. The problems of educationally backward children were however being studied, notably by Burt (1937) and Schonell (1942), the latter quoting figures of 10 to 15 per cent of children with poor basic attainments and drawing attention in particular to the needs of children who were poor in reading, writing and spelling in spite of being intelligent enough. As a result of this pre-war research, when ten categories of handicapped children were defined following the 1944 Education Act, a category was defined *the educationally subnormal*, which was intended to refer to the broad group of educationally handicapped children who, it was suggested, formed about 10 per cent of the school population. It was envisaged that about 1 per cent of children might require 'special educational treatment' in a special school. In a Ministry of Education pamphlet in 1946 it was suggested that how arrangements for the other 8 or 9 per cent of children with learning difficulties should be made in ordinary schools was a matter for experiment:

> There is as yet no unanimity of view on how schools can make the best arrangements for their retarded children. In the past, arrangements for dealing with dull and backward children has been made on the assumption that there were few of them, and that something makeshift might serve their purpose. It is now realized that there are many, probably as many as are suitable for grammar school education, and something at once more

permanent and more carefully considered is needed (Ministry of Education, 1946).

The story since then has indeed been one of experiment and gradual development of provision for the least successful. Nearly 30 years afterwards, an impression of the ways schools organized special help for low achievers was obtained by a survey undertaken for the Bullock Committee (DES, 1975) which was inquiring into the teaching of English. In primary schools, virtually all the poorest readers among six-year-olds were said to read to their teachers daily or at least three or four times a week and this was almost as true for nine-year-olds. How effective this is, of course, depends on how well the teachers are able to recognize and help children over their difficulties; the report, in fact, questions whether the best use was made of this reading to teacher. Three-quarters of the primary and middle schools surveyed had at least one group – and on average four groups – for poor readers withdrawn for special help, the size of group averaging six. Twelve per cent of the primary schools organized a special class.

In secondary schools, 12 per cent of 12-year-olds and 5 per cent of 14-year-olds were assessed as needing help and were said to be receiving it. Various methods of organization were employed (Table 1).

Table 1: Percentage of schools using different methods of special provision

	12-year-olds	14-year-olds
Withdrawal of individuals or small groups	63	42
Extraction groups, stable for at least a term	26	12
Remedial classes for part of the curriculum	17	13
Remedial classes or streams with most of their work in these classes	52	37

More than half of the schools used mixed ability grouping in the first year and about a third for third year, but some schools did not include children having remedial help.

Statistics are not normally collected about the number of children receiving help in special teaching groups and classes organized informally by schools but the Warnock Report was able to quote a figure of 500,000 children being so provided for, that is, 4.7 per cent of the school population. Most of the children in these classes had learning difficulties or emotional and behaviour difficulties and the majority spent less than half their time in the classes.

The help that can be organized within the school or class is obviously an important matter for pupils' capacity to benefit from schoolwork. It is also relevant to the question whether the most severely educationally retarded can be provided for in the ordinary school or are deemed to need placement in a special school. Such provision for 'educationally subnormal children' increased considerably during the period following the 1944 Education Act. Whereas the few pre-war special schools for backward children were mainly in the large towns, new schools were established in most areas.

In 1983, when a new Education Act came into force, there were 55,000 children ascertained under the previous arrangements as 'educationally subnormal'. There were 7,600 in special classes in ordinary schools and 2,400 registered in ordinary classes. This represents somewhat less than 1 per cent of the school population. There were also 30,000 mentally handicapped children in special schools.

Remedial teaching

In addition to the increased efforts made by schools on behalf of slow learners, the period from the 1944 Act to the present time saw the development of services to assist schools. One of these developed from the concept of remedial teaching. It is difficult to find any mention of the term in pre-war years although psychologists in the few child guidance clinics at that time sometimes gave remedial teaching to children referred for emotional and behaviour difficulties. In 1948, Schonell followed up his work on learning difficulties by establishing at Birmingham the first university course for training remedial teachers whom he envisaged as being appointed to schools and local education authorities to teach individuals or groups in order to remedy their poor attainments. The development of remedial education, its uncertainties and controversies, has been described fully by Sampson (1975). At the present time almost every local education authority has a remedial education service, sometimes as an autonomous service, sometimes as part of the School Psychological Service. A variety of modes of operation has developed: assistance within schools by teaching groups of retarded readers; individual or small group teaching of children attending a remedial centre part-time; advice to schools on methods for identifying, assessing and providing for educationally retarded children; in-service training by means of short courses and advice on methods and resources following up surveys in schools. The future direction in their work is likely to be in the ways of giving support to teachers as they provide for children with special needs in ordinary classes rather more than some of their traditional roles.

In the course of time, the term remedial teacher became widely applied to teachers in schools who were working either part-time or full-time to give remedial teaching to educationally retarded children. The Bullock Committee reported that 69 per cent of those teaching groups of children withdrawn for remedial help in primary schools were part-time teachers, many of whom had no recent experience of teaching reading and no in-service training for doing so. In secondary schools, the term remedial began to be applied to the teachers who were responsible for classes of low achievers and to the classes and departments catering for them. A survey of work with slow learners in secondary schools (DES, 1971) commented on the uncertainty and confusion about curricular aims with slow learners which seemed to arise from this use of the word remedial – which in essence was concerned with remedying weaknesses in basic skills rather than the planning of the broad educational programme.

Conception of the purpose, nature and effects of remedial teaching have also evolved. In the early years of its development, there was an assumption that backwardness in reading could be remedied by regular remedial teaching over a period. It was certainly easy to demonstrate that substantial gains were made and children's attitudes and adjustment improved but evaluation studies were rather less encouraging particularly over the maintenance of an improved rate of learning. The Bullock Report pointed to some of the possible reasons for this: children are sometimes returned to general class work without the level of reading competence needed for making independent progress; they need continuing support; closer liaison is needed between remedial teachers and class teachers. One may add to this the fact that some children have difficulties which continue to affect their learning across the curriculum.

The Bullock Report clearly expressed the view that remedial help should be closely related to the child's work in class and that every primary teacher should plan a reading programme designed to cater for all levels of ability in the class. In secondary schools, the committee pointed to ways in which withdrawal for remedial help might be minimized and co-operation between remedial teachers and other teachers could help to relate remedial help to the rest of the pupils' work.

Remedial teachers had themselves realized that the problems of children with low attainments in basic educational skills were not necessarily resolved by short periods of remedial teaching several times a week; moreover, that it would be unrealistic to expect enough remedial teachers to be appointed to give additional help to all those children who might benefit from it. All teachers, at whatever level of schooling or whatever their specialist field or subject of teaching, have the main responsibility for teaching pupils whether they are high or low achievers. Remedial teaching is an additional resource – both for remedial teaching and advice to other teachers about methods and materials – not only in relation to learning of basic skills but also of other subjects.

This view was very clearly stated in a report on the education of children with learning difficulties (Scottish Education Department, 1978):

Because the range of learning difficulties is so wide and their nature so complex, it is too much to ask that they be tackled by the provision of remedial teachers alone.

Thus remedial education is a responsibility of the whole school whether remedial staff are employed or not.

Pupils with learning difficulties should be taught as far as possible by class and subject teachers. If they are unable to give the proper kind of help, then the pupils involved should be given the additional support of a remedial teacher. That fact, however, does not reduce the class or subject teacher's responsibility for the pupils or absolve him from continuing his own endeavours.

The School Psychological Service

Another source of help which developed during the post-war period was the School Psychological Service which is staffed by educational psychologists. In addition to having qualifications in psychology, they are qualified teachers who, after teaching experience, have taken a further course of training in educational psychology. Their expertise is relevant to many aspects of educational practice but their major allocation of time is given to children and young people with special needs and to advice and co-operation with teachers. They are not, as is sometimes thought, simply concerned with assessment and the use of testing procedures. They see their role rather as helping teachers in the assessment of children's educational and adjustment needs with a view to developing teaching programmes and treatment approaches in schools. It has been recommended that there should be one educational psychologist to every 5,000 pupils; in Scotland a ratio of 1:3000 has been achieved. It would be unrealistic to expect educational psychologists to be involved in all the problems that might arise in that number of children, especially as they are expected to be involved with pre-school children and with the post-16 age group. Psychologists are therefore keen to develop a preventative role: the early identification of children with special needs in an area or within a school; collaborative projects with teachers which help to modify the organization and approach of schools so that problems are less likely to become severe and can be more productively tackled (Gillham, 1978).

Support services

There are also peripatetic advisory teachers who are specialists in particular disabilities. A service of teachers of the hearing impaired provides support for hearing impaired children 55 per cent of whom are in ordinary schools. A similar service in respect of visually handicapped children has developed during the 1970s since more blind and partially sighted children are being educated in ordinary schools, either in special units or ordinary classes. There are also home visiting teachers who work with children convalescing after hospital treatment or unable to go to school for other reasons.

Close liaison with child health services – doctors, health visitors, speech therapists and other specialists as needed – is an important aspect of provision for children with educational and other difficulties. On the social aspect, the Educational Social Work Service is a first source of information and action in respect of pupils at school and there is also likely to be Social Services involvement. Communication with and between these services, co-ordination and co-operation are obviously highly desirable. In the school years, the teachers are well placed to recognize the need for their help and to co-ordinate efforts.

Although these advisory and support services have developed and more provision for low achieving children in ordinary and special schools has been made, there must be dissatisfaction with the slow and incomplete progress that has been made. We cannot guarantee that a slow pupil or a failing pupil gets sufficient help nor be sure how to educate them in spite of their basic difficulties. That greater progress has not been made may partly be due to the many other preoccupations of schools during the last three decades. It has been a period of continued change both in education and society as a whole. Schools have adjusted to the school leaving age being raised on two occasions; the secondary school system has been reorganized on comprehensive lines; curricula and forms of organization within schools have been redeveloped; schools have had to respond to new needs arising from population changes and in general to a changing society with new problems, attitudes and expectations. Some would say that the low achiever has been low in the order of priorities, although some would consider that to be more true of the average and slightly below average group.

List of further reading

PRITCHARD, D. (1960). *Education and the Handicapped*. London: Routledge and Kegan Paul.
WARNOCK REPORT. Chap. 2. The Historical Background.

CHAPTER 2
The New Framework

The Warnock Report

In the late 1960s and early 70s, there was a growing dissatisfaction with the provision of special help for handicapped children as well as for children with learning and other difficulties in schools. There were several reasons for this. There were the results of the survey quoted earlier which showed that the number of children with educational and other difficulties was much greater than the small number for whom provision was made in special schools. There was unease about the system of placing children into ten categories of handicap for special schooling according to their major disability since children often have additional handicaps and broader personal needs – categories tended to lead to a restricted view of their needs. There was also a strong current of opinion in Britain and other countries that methods of organizing special help – particularly by placement in special schools but also by special arrangements in ordinary schools – should not set children apart from other pupils; their education and experience of schooling should be as normal as possible. There was also the sense that the expertise of the various professions – medical, educational, social – concerned with the education and welfare of children could be better co-ordinated to provide continuity of assessment and provision from infancy to late adolescence. A government committee of inquiry (the Warnock Committee) was set up in 1974 to review educational provision 'for children and young people handicapped by disabilities of body or mind' and 'to consider the most effective use of resources' and 'to make recommendations'.

The Warnock Report was published in 1978 (Department of Education and Science) and made more than 200 recommendations. A short version of the committee views was also published (Warnock, 1978).

A basic conclusion of the report was that a distinction between handicapped and non-handicapped children was untenable as was the assumption that the handicapped needed special education and the non-handicapped ordinary education. They proposed the term *special educational needs*, which takes into account children's aptitudes and other qualities as well as disabilities, and which points to *needs* for such things as special teaching, resources and facilities, possibly a modified or special curriculum and special attention to the social and emotional climate of the school or class. It is thus a more positive approach directing attention towards the kinds of special help required by children rather than referring to their disabilities and handicaps although these as well as many other individual characteristics have to be taken into account in defining needs.

A further recommendation was that services should be based on the assumption that 'about one in six children at any time and up to one in five children at some time during their school career will require some form of special help'. The conclusion that 15 to 20 per cent of children might be deemed to have special educational needs seemed surprising to many people; the education service was accustomed to a situation in which about 2 per cent of children were placed in special schools. The recommendation was, however, reasonably based on the findings of the National Child Development Study (Kellmer Pringle *et al.*, 1966), the Isle of Wight survey (Rutter *et al.*, 1970) and several other estimates, including those based on teachers' judgements.

The implications of these recommendations were that we should not conceive special education as synonymous with special *schooling*. The report defined special education in terms of what it consists of, irrespective of where it is provided:

(i)   *effective access on a full- or part-time basis to teachers with appropriate qualifications or substantial experience or both.* The term 'effective access' is broad enough to include the large numbers of cases where a child is in an ordinary class but may be withdrawn for special help or his or her teachers may obtain help, advice and resources from an advisory or consultant teacher with experience or training in teaching children with learning difficulties or sensory, physical or other disabilities.

(ii) *effective access on a full- or part-time basis to other professionals with appropriate training.* This would include educational psychologists, speech therapists or other therapists, doctors, nurses, social workers and others.

(iii) *an educational and physical environment with the necessary aids, equipment and resources appropriate to the child's special needs.* The committee had in mind such things as the many modifications which enable a physically handicapped child to get around a school building; equipment which will enable him or her to take part in normal classwork; equipment which enables the hearing impaired child to hear better and the visually handicapped to use printed books and representational material or to use Braille and the resources developed for the education of blind children. For educationally retarded children, there are many technical resources as well as suitable books and teaching programmes, often placed in a special resources room.

The committee was thus emphasizing that special education should be defined in terms of what it consists of, not where it takes place. It underlines the importance of developing and improving the methods and organization for children with special needs in ordinary schools, the need for which is all the more important in view of the committee's support for the principle of integration, i.e. that so far as possible children with special needs should be educated in ordinary schools.

Integration, or mainstreaming as it is called in the USA, does not mean that *all* children with special needs should be educated in the ordinary school. The Warnock Report recorded the view that, alongside a move in the direction of educating a greater proportion of handicapped children in ordinary schools, special schools will continue to feature in the range of provision for children with special needs. That range includes education in an ordinary class with help and support or with periods of withdrawal to a special class or unit or other supporting base; education in a special class or unit with periods of attendance in ordinary classes; full-time education in a special class or unit with social contact with the main school. Education in a special school may involve some academic experience and social contact with an ordinary school. The American concept of mainstreaming employs the idea of 'the least restrictive environment', i.e. the child is placed in a setting which is appropriate to their needs but with the aim of moving them closer to a normal setting as it becomes possible.

In their discussion of integration, the Warnock Committee distinguished between locational, social and functional (or academic) integration. Locating a special class in an ordinary school or a special school on the same campus as an ordinary school is a step towards integration. There are possibilities for social and functional integration. Social integration may occur incidentally but is likely to need to be promoted and encouraged by teachers. Academic integration depends partly on whether the children are ready to benefit from participation in lessons in the ordinary school. Even if they are ready to do so, it depends also on the readiness of teachers to accept them in their classes. In practice, integration depends on positive attitudes in teachers and also on practical matters such as class size, the availability of help and advice to teachers and their understanding of how to provide for a wide range of ability and achievement. There are now many examples of successful schemes of integration (Hegarty and Pocklington with Lucas, 1981, 1982).

The Warnock Committee made recommendations about a wide range of other issues: the importance of early recognition of special needs and continuity of provision from pre-school through the school years to the post-school years. It emphasized three main areas as priorities for better provision: the pre-school years in which much can be done to assist children's development so that they are better prepared for the normal school years; the post-school years during which further education and a vocational element can prepare them for work and life in the community; teacher training since the Warnock conception of special educational provision requires more teachers with specialist training for teaching children with special needs, especially in integrated settings. Moreover, all teachers in their initial training should have a better preparation for helping such children. The Warnock Report also stressed the importance of co-operation with parents, of co-operation and co-ordination between the professional specialists involved and of improved support and advisory services for teachers.

The Education Act 1981

Some of the main recommendations of the Warnock Report were embodied in the Education Act 1981 which came into force in April 1983. The Act requires local education authorities to provide for children with special educational needs and states that a child has special educational needs if they have a learning difficulty significantly greater than the majority of children of their age or have a mental or physical disability which prevents or hinders them from making use of the educational facilities generally provided. A learning difficulty which arises solely because the language of the home is different from that of the school is specifically excluded.

There is no mention in the Act of particular disabilities and it therefore replaces the 1944 Education Act's system of classifying children for special education according to ten categories of handicap. It is the responsibility of ordinary schools to recognize and provide for the majority of children with special needs but in the case of a small proportion of children whose education is likely to need provision additional to, or different from the facilities and resources generally available under normal arrangements, the local authority has to arrange a formal assessment procedure to give the child the protection of a *statement* of their needs. Whereas the procedures under the 1944 Act led to placing a child in one of ten categories of handicap which in most cases led to placement in a special school or unit for children with that particular handicap, the circulars explaining the 1981 Act take pains to stress that three aspects of the assessment procedure should be clearly distinguished.

First, the analysis of the child's learning difficulty – their strengths and weaknesses in physical, cognitive and language development; their educational attainment and social development; factors in the home or school environment which lessen or contribute to their needs; relevant aspects of their medical and educational history. Teachers, educational psychologists, doctors and other specialists would all contribute to this assessment. The information would be the basis of the second stage – the specification of the child's needs for special teaching, special resources and facilities. The third stage in the process is deciding what kind of special educational provision is required to meet those needs. In line with the importance given by the Warnock Report to the involvement of parents in their child's education, parents are given rights to be informed before an assessment procedure is to be instituted; their comments must be invited about the draft of the statement and at several stages they may make representations. Where appropriate the child's views should be obtained.

The procedure may appear a detailed and time-consuming one but it is designed to ensure that no aspect is neglected in assessing a child's difficulty and deciding his or her needs. The optimum co-operation and communication between the professional specialists involved, and with the parents, is also aimed for. Sayer (1983a), the headmaster of a large comprehensive school, has suggested provocatively, and perhaps prophetically, that the individual statements of the 1981 Act would not be needed if a school were committed to providing for all children and a local authority were committed to resourcing the school to do so. The 'if clause' in that sentence should be seen as a challenge to the next generation of teachers, teacher trainers and administrators. We should aim for the next step in 'normalizing' the education of children with special needs by making it part of normal professional procedures. At least the Act has removed any terminology referring to particular 'types' of children other than the broad one of special educational needs. We should also try in practice to avoid or minimize the use of terms which act as labels for classes or types of children which tend to limit our perception of their individuality. Likewise, ways of providing special help of various kinds should become, so far as possible, part of the general process in schools of providing for children's special interests, abilities, difficulties and needs.

In the comparable American requirements under Public Law 94–142, the Education for All Handicapped Children Act, an individualized educational programme (the IEP) must be developed at a meeting attended by a representative of the local educational agency, the child's teachers, parents and, as appropriate, the child. The IEP must specify the annual goals and short-term objectives, the special services to be provided, their starting dates and projected duration, the extent of expected participation in normal class work, as well as objective criteria and evaluation procedures whereby progress in achieving instructional objectives can be reviewed annually. Pocklington (1980) refers to initial turmoil as the legislation was implemented, followed by evidence of beneficial results.

The specification of an individualized educational programme in the detail outlined is based on a model of teaching to schemes and progressions of instructional objectives. While this type of approach has had some influence in England, it is far from universal and would be regarded by many teachers as running counter to their own view of the teaching process. Wedell *et al.* (1982) suggest several practical reasons why a prescriptive approach would not be feasible and they suggest that the main justification for making a statement is one of accountability – to the child and his or her parents, to the local authority, community and taxpayer – for the provisions and additional resources required to meet the child's special needs.

Assessment

The concept of special educational needs has considerable implications for the assessment of children. DES Circular 1/83, which offered advice to LEAs, emphasized that 'the main focus should be on the child himself rather than on his disability since the extent to which a learning difficulty hinders a child's development depends not only on the nature and severity of the difficulty but also on the personal resources and attributes of the child and on the help and support he receives at home and school. A child's special educational needs are thus related to his abilities as well as his disabilities and to the nature of his interaction with his environment'.

In other words, the assessment process is not simply concerned with establishing how retarded the child is in their attainments nor with the nature of their difficulties but with an understanding of the child as a person who has potentialities and strengths as well as difficulties and whose development is influenced by the quality of support from school and home. Assessment is a process which identifies possibilities for change and also involves the process of monitoring change. It is appropriate therefore that the circular should emphasize that assessment 'is not a single event but a continuous process' and that 'where the interventions made at school do not seem to meet the child's needs, further investigation will be required'.

The circular stresses that assessment requires a partnership between parents, teachers and other professionals in a joint endeavour to discover and understand the nature of the difficulties and needs of the child. Teachers and parents, especially in the case of younger children, are more commonly in communication than formerly. But there are times when parents are unaware of children's difficulties and, conversely, sometimes parents believe there is a problem and the teacher may not. Sometimes their impressions complement each other and contribute to better understanding of the child. Where parents can be involved in some form of help, anxieties and unproductive responses may be avoided.

The circular also makes the important recommendation that the feelings and perceptions of the child should be taken into account and that the concept of partnership should wherever possible be extended to older children and young persons. What we may believe to be the best form of help for older pupils is less likely to prove so if they have not been given and accepted the reasons for it.

With regard to other professionals the circular refers to the need for effective lines of communication between teachers and various specialists including the school doctor and nurse to ensure that the teacher is informed of the implications of health and other problems. The Educational Social Work Service may also be able to inform schools about matters relevant to children's response to school. Physical and health factors should not be overlooked. Respiratory conditions may result in absences and proneness to fatigue. Epileptic conditions may have no observable consequences but the possible effects of sedation and the possibility of underfunctioning should be recognized. A mild hearing impairment may be intermittent and unidentified; a visual impairment may have educational significance; a degree of speech and language disorder may require assessment by a speech therapist; mild physical disabilities, clumsiness and difficulties in hand-eye co-ordination may contribute to a learning difficulty. Factors in the home such as illness, bereavements, separations and other potential sources of anxiety in the family or the child require sensitive watchfulness so that teachers respond helpfully as well as recognizing possible effects on learning and adjustment.

The Warnock Report referred to five stages of assessment, the first three being school based and the other two going beyond the school, involving various kinds of specialist assessment in centres, clinics or hospitals. School-based assessment starts with a class teacher's observation of a learning difficulty, leading to a wider consultation within the school – the headteacher or senior teachers, a teacher with responsibility for special educational needs or visiting teachers from the advisory or support services. The educational psychologist or personnel from health and social services may be consulted. At some stage, the parents would be involved in discussion of the child's needs. In a few cases (see p.19), when it is thought that the child's needs require special forms of help different from those generally available, the child would be referred to a formal assessment which might lead to the preparation of a statement of their needs.

Assessment in school

The school's knowledge of the child is most important at every stage. Even if assessment goes beyond the school, what the teacher has to say in written reports (or better still in case conference) is valuable information which confirms or sheds a different light on what others have to say. Schools employ a variety of ways of assessing pupils' progress, the basic one being records of children's progress in different areas of the curriculum and the informal observations which all teachers make as children are being taught. Observation depends, of course, on knowing what to look for and this derives, first, from an understanding of the sequence of skills, concepts and knowledge which have been identified in particular curriculum areas, and, secondly, from teachers' experience of where children often have difficulties in understanding and learning.

But as Circular 1/83 emphasized, the nature and severity of a child's learning difficulty and needs cannot properly be assessed without viewing the child as a whole: their ability to concentrate and persist – which may vary according to the tasks; their attitude to success and failure; their levels of thinking and understanding as shown in their interests and in many classroom experiences; their ability to comprehend language and to express themselves; their co-ordination in physical activities and in classroom tasks requiring fine control; their emotional maturity and adjustment and their social adjustment in relation to other children, adults and family. It is often difficult to decide how far certain characteristics are causative factors in the learning failure or are a consequence of it. Monitoring the effects of measures to improve learning, to create and reward success, to improve acceptance within classroom groups or to promote positive home support often help to elucidate the nature and degree of the learning difficulty.

It is worth noting that teachers' conceptions of what is 'normal' for a particular age or stage is likely to be influenced by previous experience of groups of children and that also the seriousness of a learning difficulty may be viewed differently according to the intake and the expectations of particular schools. This is where the opinion of an experienced teacher, an advisory teacher or educational psychologist would be helpful. Sometimes a less experienced teacher feels insecure and inadequate in teaching children with marked special needs. The essential first step is to communicate acceptance and a concern to tackle their difficulties – whether in learning or adjustment. It is a rewarding experience when the signs of change begin to appear.

In teaching children with learning difficulties, the teacher needs what may be termed a *diagnostic* approach. For example, the sample on p. 25 of an 11-year-old's writing looks very poor and would be likely to attract negative comments. But we may note first some positive features. He has something to say and he has persisted in the attempt to say it. Moreover, some of the crossing out and several attempts at words indicate that he is aware of mistakes and tries to correct them. Leaving aside the misspellings of names, his errors are:

graet (great); scoed (scored); four (for); goll (goal); frend (friend); maniger (manager). There are two cases where the final *t* is written as *ed* (beased, lased). There are three cases where an *h* has been added at the beginning of a word – reflecting a local pronunciation.

A first step would be to teach him a method of learning spellings (see p. 121) and to check how successfully he learns them and retains them over a period.

A bad woltk workswores

Wolwoves

Wolves is a graet team. but I like waned woll
the best but, ande grey hes left and Wane dour hus
left by my b foot ball ffem team is lanehead strois
We play Some mor mo more teams. lastel
Satday we wun Five to One fous und we go
training on theso Mondagy My mareiger
is Naid named Ted we play to Ten a Side
and Sometimes we have all a side with more hour
I have scoed a goll hand My frend calledLee hus
scoed 3 goils goll the best beasdinhour
team is Shan and Lee we play in there in a
proper team wreawhen I ham older I ham going to
play four woves or Spis Tottnham Tot nham.

A second step would be attention to his writing. Many individual letters are quite well formed. He does not seem to have been taught or has not learned how to make joins – although there are some examples of satisfactory joins. Some reteaching and some appropriate incentives and rewards for improved writing are likely to bring about an improvement which would bring the further rewards of greater success in other schoolwork.

A similar diagnostic approach in listening to children read can reveal information about phonic elements which the child does not know, about speed of reading and about comprehension. The analysis of miscues (see p. 119) is a simple procedure for evaluating the extent to which the reader uses grapho-phonemic, semantic and syntactic cues as they read.

In many situations, getting a child to explain a process or concept can be revealing, for example, verbalizing a mathematical activity or process may reveal an underlying misconception.

Normative tests of attainments and abilities are so-called because performance can be compared with norms obtained by the test constructors from a representative sample of children of the age groups for whom the test was designed. Such tests are therefore appropriate when we wish to compare children with a common standard, for example, when pupils enter secondary schools from a number of feeder schools and come with reports based on various forms of assessment or results from different tests of attainment. On occasions, a school or an education authority may wish to compare attainments with a national standard. Some norm referenced tests are also designed to yield diagnostic information, for example different facets of reading comprehension or mathematical ability.

Recent normative tests have been constructed on the basis of a sophisticated methodology: for the selection and rejection of items; for establishing the validity of the test (that it measures what it purports to) and its reliability (that it does not give very different results on another occasion). It is still necessary for teachers to examine what the test is testing to see whether it matches their conception of the particular attainment. A cautionary note is that some tests still in use are rather old; they may not have been constructed to modern standards and the content, vocabulary and conception of the attainment may be questionable.

The scores on normative tests of intelligence or attainment used to be expressed as mental or attainment ages or as quotients. Scores are now generally expressed as standard scores, usually with a mean of 100 and a standard deviation of 15 (i.e. the spread of scores around the mean). Comparison of performance on several such tests can thus be legitimately made.

Criterion referenced testing involves no comparison with the performance of other people but is simply concerned with establishing whether a particular skill or item of knowledge has been learnt to a specified criterion. The driving test is an example. The tester is not concerned to put you on a scale from very good to poor but simply to say whether you reach a satisfactory level of competence. Many vocational and craft skills are assessed in a similar way. Competence in social and self-care skills (e.g. dressing, eating, independence) have for a long time been assessed in this way with young children or retarded pupils. Schedules defining steps in the sequence of development in young children are another example. In further education, use is being made of profiles which include criteria for performance in social and vocational skills.

Criterion referenced assessment has come to the fore in recent years in connection with attempts to define curricula in terms of behavioural objectives. The objectives are defined precisely as the behaviour which is the intended outcome of instruction, together with the conditions under which it is performed, e.g. the speed of performance, the materials or setting, etc. Failure or difficulty may indicate the need to analyse the task into smaller steps. Criterion referenced assessment is thus integrally related to learning providing both the teacher and the learner with knowledge of results.

When learning can be sequenced and its stages clearly defined, criterion referenced testing has application and is a means of frequent (perhaps daily) checking on progress rather than waiting to the end of the term or year to give a normative test to see whether attainments have improved. A refinement of this procedure is precision-teaching in which there is regular recording of progress by means of short tests or probes, the results being graphed. The information may indicate the need for change in the teaching – changing the materials or method; analysing the skill into easier steps (Raybould and Solity, 1982; Muncey and Williams, 1981).

Motivation for learning

Assessment involves observation of children's attitude and approach to learning including their motivation. Even though the children are less intelligent, less verbal, less well adjusted, unsettled by factors in their lives outside school or affected by a disability of some kind, if their attitudes towards and motivation for learning are positive, the teacher can anticipate a measure of success.

There are, of course, many ways of looking at attitude and motivation but a simple example will illustrate. Hewitt (1964) distinguished several levels of motivation, the last four being the exploratory level, the relationship level, the mastery level and the achievement level. In the infant school after an initial period of adjustment to school, we would hope to see signs of the *exploratory* level, i.e. learning through engagement in the activities and interests of the infant classroom leading towards the beginning of school learning. There are children whose withdrawal, social isolation or hyperactive behaviour do not permit them to respond at this level and the teacher would be concerned to encourage and reward steps towards participation and social interaction.

Sooner rather than later, teachers would look for signs of a responsive *relationship* between teacher and child and also that the child was becoming part of the class group or small friendship groups. They would seek ways of helping the child to relate to themselves and to interact with other children. Subsequently, teachers would look for signs of the *mastery* level where children want to master skills for themselves and, through small realizable goals, obtain success. At the primary stage, this is a major need of children. Erikson (1965) in an interesting account of the phases of personal development has described the period from ages 7 to 11 as one of 'acquiring a sense of industry and fending off a sense of inferiority' and considers that many of the later attitudes towards work and work habits can be traced to a degree of successful effort and sense of achievement at these stages. If there is little success in learning tasks, it is important that other achievements can compensate. At the final stage, the *achievement* task level, the child or adolescent is fairly consistently self-motivated, anticipates success and has begun to see long-term goals for school learning.

The critical factor in moving through these stages is the nature of the rewards, a fact which teachers recognize by providing activities, materials, group situations, approval and praise appropriate to the level of the child's maturity. A significant feature of learning failure is that rewards may be few compared with those the successful learner obtains. The effects of well-sequenced work linked with systematic rewards have been shown in many studies. Glynn *et al.* (1978), for example, were able to bring about significant change in the learning and morale of a special class of educationally retarded children by rewarding completion of learning tasks by a period of time in an adjacent play area.

List of further reading

BRENNAN, W.K. (1982). *Changing Special Education*. Milton Keynes: Open University Press.
WARNOCK, M. (1978). *Special Educational Needs: a brief guide to the Warnock Report*. London: HMSO.
NEWELL, P. *The New Law on Children with Special Needs*. London: Advisory Centre for Education.
VARIOUS CONTRIBUTORS (1978). The Warnock Report: its contents and contexts. *Special Education: Forward Trends, 5*, 3.

CHAPTER 3
The Nature and Sources of Learning Difficulties

The figure of a dunce in a dunce's cap standing in the corner of the classroom used to occur in children's books and comics. If that situation had reality in actual classrooms, it is difficult to imagine what teachers thought the practice would achieve and what beliefs they had about failure in learning. Presumably they had little understanding of the differences in children's abilities to learn and no appreciation of the negative effects of shame in reducing pupils' self-esteem or in stoking up hostility to school. We cannot, however, be complacent since although we don't put the dunce in the corner, there are other inadequacies in our practice. We are still engaged in the process of understanding learning difficulty and how the organization and practices of schools can avoid or minimize its negative effects in a society where achievement and success are highly valued – and perhaps too narrowly defined.

Understanding of learning difficulties has been developing only gradually from the time when education became compulsory and all children came to school. A headteacher's entry in a school log book on 27 January 1879 read 'I have thoroughly examined the newcomers. I find about half the number can be decently prepared for Standard 1. About 12 or 14 cannot say their letters and as to their writing, they have no notion of writing from a copy to say nothing of writing from a book or card.' On 4 February the teacher recorded: 'I have taken Standard 1 again this week. What to do with about 20 of them I am at a loss to know' (Ingram, 1958). At that time the medical profession was the only one with knowledge and interest in children's physical, sensory and mental disabilities; indeed the first descriptions of children with severe reading problems (which they termed 'word blindness') were made by doctors before 1900. It is significant that until 1932 the Board of Education inspector responsible for handicapped pupils was a medical man. It is not surprising therefore that a medical approach to the definition and classification of educational handicaps was influential, as was the tendency to look for their causes within the pupil rather more than in the way he or she was being taught. Legislation in 1921 defined five types of 'defective' children and the number was further increased following the Education Act of 1944 when ten categories of handicapped children were defined as requiring special educational treatment. Subsequently, increasing disquiet about the constricting effects of categories on professional thinking and practice led to their abolition by the Education Act of 1981. Their replacement by the term, special educational needs, may be seen as a significant shift from a medical model focusing on deficiencies and definable conditions to an educational conception recognizing the complex variety of individual, environmental and school factors giving rise to pupils' educational and personal needs. It will no doubt take time to overcome the tendency to view learning difficulties as conditions comparable to the clinical entities of medicine and to achieve a balance between recognizing pupils' difficulties and identifying their needs.

The ground for this has, however, been prepared by other disciplines which successively became involved – and of course by developments in educational theory and practice. Psychology as an academic discipline with practical applications is mainly a development of this century. The 'invention' of objective tests of abilities and attainments was an early and useful advance on previous impressionistic methods even though they are now seen to have been rather over-emphasized and often used within a medical model of learning difficulties. From a too exclusive concern with pupils' abilities and disabilities, educational psychology has increasingly moved into the study of the factors in the school and home influencing children's development, the study of learning and adjustment processes and the organization and management of learning – the interactions between the learner, the learning tasks and the school and class settings in which they take place. This trend is reflected in the changing role of professional educational psychologists. Whereas they used to be mainly concerned with individual children, they are now as much concerned with the teachers' problems in recognizing and teaching children with learning difficulties and how teaching and organization can alleviate difficulties.

A complementary influence has been the sociology of education. Whereas the doctor and the psychologist have primarily been concerned with individuals, the sociologist forces us to consider how we conceive and define – even create and perpetuate – failure in the context of the social structure and value systems of schools and of society generally. It has provided insights which challenge existing concepts of learning difficulty, maladjustment and handicap and the implications of the special forms of provision made for them. While we have tended to assume that classificatory terminology and special provisions have been developed to benefit children, sociology prompts us to consider whether they serve the function of maintaining the orderly running of schools and society (Tomlinson, 1982).

While the knowledge and insight derived from these and other specialist fields (such as social work, speech therapy and physiotherapy) contribute to the understanding of and provision for children with special needs, the solutions which teachers must look for are educational ones: what should we aim to teach? how should we teach it? how should schools and classrooms be organized and run to ensure effective teaching of all pupils? Teaching is a practical activity involving a considerable range of skills and understandings; it is not easy to theorize about it in the overwhelmingly busy activity of daily teaching. It is easy therefore for teachers to be over-impressed by external influences or the latest new idea or fashion and to underestimate the knowledge and understanding they acquire through the close experience of teaching individuals and classes. Much can be gained from the stimulus of other conceptions and the help of other expertise but the heart of the matter is trying to teach a child who is hard to teach – and learning from the experience.

Degrees of learning difficulty

In accordance with the changes in concepts which have been outlined, the 1981 Act and its related circulars employed no terms to refer to particular groups of children with special needs. To have done so would have tended to perpetuate classification and labelling of children. In everyday practice we do, of course, need words to refer to particular disabilities and difficulties. In some cases such terms carry useful connotations. For example, visually impaired or hearing impaired imply the need for special teaching methods, materials, resources and aids and the importance of specially qualified teachers. Other terms such as physically handicapped have less precise connotations because the variety of disabilities and their consequences covered by the term mean that the implications are less predictable. In the case of learning difficulties – the most frequent source of special needs – the variety of interacting factors involved is so great and extends over such a range of learning performance from more or less average to very much below average that it would be difficult to make generalizations about the teaching and resources required.

The Warnock Report suggested that learning difficulties might be described as *mild, moderate* or *severe*. Significantly, these terms were proposed in a chapter on curricular issues and they are essentially curriculum distinctions. Thus, it was suggested that children with a *mild* learning difficulty can successfully be helped to follow the normal curriculum and 'indeed the majority will be able to manage, with appropriate support, in ordinary classes.' Appropriate support includes remedial teaching and also teaching which takes account of their difficulty in mastering complex ideas; 'many require persistent personal support and encouragement if they are to make progress.'

Moderate learning difficulties stem from a variety and combination of causes which often include mild and multiple physical and sensory difficulties, limited general ability and adverse social and educational experiences. The need for a somewhat different curriculum was indicated by the committee's recommendation that 'particular attention should be given to curriculum development for children with moderate learning difficulties.'

The learning difficulties of children who have generally been referred to as mentally handicapped were termed *severe*. Their retarded development requires a curriculum which aims to develop their independence, social skills, language and other aspects of development 'by means of precisely analysed and small incremental objectives.'

Official support for this approach is shown in a DES form on which LEAs make a statistical return about the number of children assessed for or receiving special education. On one dimension, children are recorded according to one of three curriculum types (mainstream with support, modified, developmental) and on a second dimension they are recorded according to whether they have any disabilities (physical, epilepsy, communication difficulties, visual or hearing impairments, or behaviour/social difficulties). The normal curriculum or '*mainstream with support*' is described as 'a curriculum as provided in ordinary schools but with the provision of additional support to pupils which may be in the form of additional resources e.g. aids, small group teaching, ancillary help.' A *modified* curriculum is 'similar to that provided in ordinary schools but, while not restricted in its expectations, has objectives more appropriate to children with moderate learning difficulties.' A *developmental* curriculum covers 'a range of educational experiences but more selectively and sharply focussed on the development of personal autonomy and social skills, with precisely defined objectives and designed for children with severe learning difficulties.'

It could well be suggested that this curriculum-based distinction between mild, moderate and severe difficulties is not really different from former practice in which children were ascertained as educationally subnormal (mild or severe) and given special education in the appropriate special schools or units. There is however a difference in orientation to the problem of learning difficulties. Previously, attention tended to be directed towards pupils' limitations and difficulties (which were easily taken to imply a particular type or category of child) whereas the new formulation directs attention to the child's curricular needs. The alternatives of a mainstream curriculum with support and a modified curriculum put the emphasis on the curriculum and also pose the question what each of them means in practice. For example, what does mainstream *with support* mean? – a question which will be considered later. How far may the normal curriculum and the methods of teaching it be extended to encompass the needs of some children who might otherwise be deemed to need a modified curriculum? How different is a modified curriculum so that while being similar to the normal curriculum, it has objectives more appropriate to children with moderate learning difficulties?

The terms mild, moderate and severe learning difficulties – especially the latter two – have become current usage although there is no statutory basis for them. It is important to keep in mind that they refer to degrees of difficulty in learning, not to clearly defined groups of children, and that they imply needs for three kinds of curriculum and appropriate teaching methods.

Severe learning difficulties

The degree of difficulty and the need for a special curriculum different from that in ordinary schools is most clear-cut in the case of severe learning difficulties. Provision for mentally handicapped children did not become a responsibility of the educational service until the Education Act 1970, which came into effect in 1971. Prior to that date, they had been considered as 'unsuitable for education' and been provided for in junior training centres under the responsibility of Health Departments. However, in the period from 1945, research and practice had demonstrated that their capacity to learn and to make progress towards social competence and independence was much greater than had previously been assumed. This, together with the support of public opinion, led to the transfer of responsibility to Education; the centres became schools and new courses were instituted to train specialist teachers.

Since then much progress has been made in developing a distinctive form of education, which has been notably assisted by research and development, for example at the Hester Adrian Centre, Manchester (Mittler, 1979). Finely graded and sequenced programmes to promote self-help, social competence, physical skills, language and communication are complemented by activities which aim to give children as normal a social and environmental experience as possible. The 28,000 pupils in schools range from the pre-school ages to late adolescence and range in degree from profound and multiple handicap to levels of achievement which include some reading ability. A few pupils are being educated in ordinary nursery and primary classes and there is a small number of special units in ordinary primary and secondary schools as well as special courses in ordinary colleges of further education (Brennan, 1982; Hegarty and Pocklington with

Lucas, 1982). Such forms of provision are likely to increase; there are already opportunities for participation in social and recreative activities with other children or young people. It is to be hoped that links between these special schools and ordinary schools will be encouraged since experience with non-handicapped children and a variety of normal situations is a desirable part of the education of children with severe difficulties as a preparation for living and being accepted in the adult community.

Moderate learning difficulties

Distinctions between severe and moderate learning difficulties cannot clearly be made at the borderline between the two and are not important so long as children with moderate difficulties are given appropriate help in areas of retarded development and those with severe difficulties are helped to acquire educational skills of which they may be capable. There are some special schools in fact which provide for both groups.

Distinguishing between moderate and mild difficulties – between those who are thought to need a modified curriculum and those who can manage a mainstream curriculum with support – is more difficult. It depends on the normal curriculum, the teaching methods employed, the organization of teaching groups and the amount and quality of additional support available. It also depends on the philosophy and ethos of the school. There are, however, pupils whose difficulties seem to require a reduced or modified curriculum, a more intensive teaching programme and – at least for a time – an adapted or supportive setting such as a special school or unit or special class can provide.

Before the 1944 Education Act, an important criterion for special school placement was, simplistically, an IQ below 70. This notion still lingers, even though many other considerations other than low ability have been taken into account. But Williams and Gruber (1967) showed that 45 per cent of a sample of 155 children in special schools for the educationally subnormal had IQs over 70; 10 per cent had IQs over 80. Marra (1981) showed that of 369 pupils in three special schools 49 per cent had IQs over 70. Clearly, many factors other than intelligence level have been involved in the judgement that children need a modified curriculum.

The Isle of Wight study (Rutter *et al.*, 1970) provides information which indicates that moderate learning difficulty is the product of an accumulation of adverse factors. This thorough multi-disciplinary research obtained information about the frequency of educational handicaps in a sample of over 3000 children aged 9 to 12 years. Fifty-seven children (2.5 per cent) had IQs below 70 on an individual test of intelligence. Only 20 of these were in a special school for moderate learning difficulties; nine were children with severe learning difficulties. The remaining half (28) were in ordinary schools. There were also seven children with IQs above 70 who had been placed in the special school. Comparing these with the children with IQs below 70 who were in ordinary schools, Rutter showed that those in the special school were 2½ to 3½ years backward in reading whereas those remaining in the ordinary school were mostly less than 2½ years backward, i.e. the degree of educational backwardness is an important element in assessing the degree of special educational need.

The importance of the degree of backwardness in reading could be one of the reasons why more boys have been placed in special schools or classes. It is usual to find that the ratio of boys to girls is 2:1. The number of boys and girls with low intelligence is roughly equal but reading backwardness (i.e. reading 2½ years below chronological age) is twice as frequent in boys than girls. Specific reading retardation (i.e. a comparison of reading level with both age and mental ability) is three times as common in boys which results in the greater number of boys than girls receiving remedial help in schools and remedial services.

The sex difference is not the only interesting one. Another factor which may have significance for teaching is that among children with mild and moderate learning difficulties there is a higher proportion of children with summer birthdays (Williams, 1964; Bookbinder, 1967). An obvious possible explanation is that such children have a shorter time in the infant or first school, i.e. infants may have two years and one term instead of three years in the infant school before moving up to the junior department. Another explanation which Bookbinder favours is that the summer-born children are always the youngest in their class or age group. This age effect is one that teachers of infant children are usually very conscious of but it perhaps needs to be considered by teachers of older age-groups. With some children, being younger and less mature may be just another factor contributing to poor progress in school.

Other information obtained by Rutter *et al.* shows that developmental delays and difficulties were more common in children with IQs below 70. Twenty-three per cent had not spoken their first words until two years of age or later, compared with only 2 per cent of the control group. At the time of the survey when children were aged between 9 and 11 years, 45 per cent still had some degree of articulation defect in speech and more than half were retarded in language development. As a group, they had been markedly delayed as babies in sitting up, walking and bladder control. At the time of assessment aged 9 to 12 years over 30 per cent had some continued co-ordination difficulties significantly greater than a control group and a definite or possible neurological abnormality was found significantly more frequently.

A survey of 916 children in special classes and schools in Cheshire (Shearer, 1977) showed the frequency of other disabilities in educationally retarded children. Seven per cent had some physical disability, 9 per cent had either a hearing or visual impairment, 20 per cent had some degree of speech disorder. The study by Marra (1981) had similar findings about speech and sensory disabilities and also reported that 17 per cent displayed some degree of poor motor co-ordination which tallies with the findings of Rutter.

It is not unexpected that several studies have reported that emotional and behaviour disorders are more common in children with moderate and mild learning difficulties than in the general school population. Chazan (1964) assessed 169 pupils (junior and seniors) from eight special schools in South Wales using the Bristol Social Adjustment Guide and found that one-third were rated as having marked emotional or behavioural difficulties. Rutter *et al.* had similar results from the intellectually handicapped in the Isle of Wight study. It is difficult to know how far these adjustment difficulties are a by-product of the developmental and health problems which have been referred to, or of adverse environmental factors or a reaction to educational failure. The important point is that such children display the need referred to in the Warnock Report (para. 3.19) for 'particular attention to the social structure and emotional climate in which education takes place.' As Chazan suggests 'a more therapeutic approach is needed'. This is in fact what special schools and classes are good at providing and it is quite common to find that children who have been unhappy or even disruptive in ordinary school settings settle happily in the more supportive and uncomplicated special environment. One of the best therapies is success – in any way at first – but particularly in educational progress.

As many other studies have done the Isle of Wight study found that the intellectually retarded were over-represented in social classes IV and V. As Rutter *et al.* point out, the reasons for this are complex. A larger number of such families suffer from economic and social deprivation; the children are more likely than other children to inherit characteristics leading to a lower level of intelligence, to experience the effect of malnutrition and to receive less good maternal care and to suffer more from the effects of childhood illnesses. The parents' own limited educational experiences may not lead to the stimulation and opportunities necessary for intellectual development.

It has been argued that special schooling may be viewed as providing education which compensates for and alleviates the effects of such social disadvantages. One might anticipate, on this view, that the aim would be to return children to the mainstream as soon as possible but this has not been happening at the rate one might expect. Fleeman (1984) followed up 33 pupils from special schools for the educationally subnormal who had been returned to ordinary schools. Over a seven-year period, this was an annual rate of transfer of only 1.1 per cent of the special school numbers. The average age of placement in the special schools was 8.6 years and of transfer was 13.2 years – it would obviously be better if transfers took place at the beginning of the secondary school. The transfer was considered to have been successful in 20 per cent of cases and fairly beneficial in 50 per cent. Some of the successful group followed CSE courses and fitted in socially quite well. Williams and Gruber (1967) gave details about 75 pupils who had been returned to ordinary schools. Their histories showed that they had experienced few of the developmental difficulties noted by Rutter *et al.* but they had experienced adverse environmental circumstances such as parental ill-health, family financial problems and inadequacies of mothering. At the point of transfer to ordinary schools, assessment of their social competence showed them to be functioning normally.

The information which has been given illustrates the statements made about moderate learning difficulties in the Warnock Report (para. 11.51): they are children 'whose difficulties stem from a variety and combination of causes. These often include mild and multiple physical and sensory disabilities, an impoverished social or educational background, specific difficulties and limited general ability.'

This variety and combination of factors in their learning difficulty show the importance of the requirements under the 1981 Education Act for an assessment of a child's difficulties by teachers, educational psychologists, doctors, social workers and where necessary by speech therapists and others with particular expertise. The assessment would not be complete without the participation of parents. The analysis of the child's difficulties is the basis for formulating needs including a judgement whether the difficulties are such that a modified curriculum is required.

What are the needs for a modified curriculum?

It is not a simple matter to distinguish and define the special needs which may require a modified curriculum. It is easy enough to point to children with retarded cognitive and language development, with difficulty in learning new skills, with personal and social immaturities, often with adjustment difficulties. They need well-planned, individualized teaching to develop their abilities and attainment; they also seem to need, at least for a time, a more secure and less demanding setting with a closer relationship to a teacher in a smaller group. Brennan (1974) referred to the need for an adaptive-developmental curriculum, indicating that their needs require some adaptation of the curriculum but also that their needs change as they mature and develop.

A modified curriculum should not be a restricted one. It should provide experience and learning which is comparable to that for other children (for example, over the eight areas of experience referred to in Chap. 5) though the content and the methods of teaching should be appropriate to their learning characteristics. It is useful to bear in mind the findings of follow-up studies of post-school progress of educationally retarded pupils. Some continue to make a limited adaptation to adult life, others have adapted reasonably well though with some degree of support from their families and others have adapted very adequately. The education we offer should be adapted to their current needs but also, as with all pupils, attempting to develop understanding and awareness for future living and work.

There are two other considerations in thinking about a modified curriculum. First, the need for it must partly be relative to the success to which a mainstream curriculum *with support* can meet the needs of pupils with learning difficulties. The nature of support and how it is provided are still open to experiment and development. Secondly, we have to consider the possibility that some pupils could be returned to the mainstream with support. As Fleeman showed, that has not been very common between special schools and ordinary schools. Special classes in ordinary schools have also often been difficult to move out from. Whether a modified curriculum is provided in an ordinary or special school, consideration should be given to its correspondence with mainstream courses.

Mild learning difficulties

The proportion of pupils who may be considered to have mild learning difficulties requiring additional help and support is much larger, perhaps 10 to 15 per cent depending how special needs are defined. The proportion also varies in different areas and schools. Mild difficulties range from those which are only marginally less severe than those just discussed to those in children whose development, adjustment and general ability are normal except for their puzzling inability in reading and writing. They may play chess, be good at sports, competent in practical tasks and, perhaps because of such compensatory successes, not suffer the lowered self-esteem and emotional reactions that are evident in so many pupils with learning difficulties.

A vast amount of research and publication has been concerned with the nature and causes of learning difficulties and many teaching methods and resources have been advocated. At various times and from different points of view, attention has focused on perceptual difficulties, memory and associative processes, laterality problems, neurological factors, speech and language difficulties, emotional and motivational factors. But as Clark (1979) concluded from a research into backward readers drawn from 1544 children aged seven in Dunbartonshire, 'the striking finding was the *diversity* of disabilities and *not* an underlying pattern to the group.' It is worth noting as well that she found that 'there was little evidence of active assistance on the part of parents... most of the children came from large families and the reading material seemed to be mainly that supplied by the school.' Absence rate was found to be associated with reading level and changes of school were common.

In view of the diversity of factors involved, generalization is hazardous but some overview is necessary. In the early years at school, there are obviously differences between children in the physical, perceptual, cognitive and language abilities involved in learning, differences also in their emotional maturity in relation to teacher, the class and the demands of learning. Once failure to learn has set in, dislike of the tasks, poor concentration and reduced confidence make learning more difficult. It is possible that remedial work may be separated from the normal experiences of the classroom; remedial work itself may over-emphasize parts of the reading process such as phonics, reducing reading to some of its elements rather than as a process for interpreting words as language expressing meanings. It is well known that some learning difficulties become very resistant to remedial treatment – which may well be due to the development of ineffective strategies.

These pupil differences are only part of the story. Clark stressed the importance of teachers' and particularly the headteachers' roles in developing a co-ordinated well-planned policy for teaching basic skills. Morris (1966) recorded the impression that, allowing for differences in pupils and circumstances, 'each school's success or failure in promoting good reading progress depended mainly on the quality of its head and staff in that order.' Having studied large samples of children in their school settings, both researchers pointed to the diversity of sources of difficulty but also to the importance of well-organized teaching. This view is reflected in the trend to put less emphasis on the pupil's difficulties and more on the nature of what has to be learnt, whether it is reading, mathematics or specialist subjects in the curriculum. Remedial work in basic skills has increasingly focused on the skills themselves and how they may be taught in such a way that progress can be frequently checked and rewarded. The scope of remedial work has widened from a narrow concern with basic skills to the broader concern of support in the curriculum as a whole. From seeing learning problems as the province of a specialist, we see all teachers as having responsibilities for the retarded learner and also have begun to involve parents at least in helping the backward reader.

The term 'mainstream with support' is an expression of this change of emphasis. So far as practicable, we aim to give children with mild learning difficulties a curriculum experience which is comparable to that of the majority of children. The word support indicates various forms of help matching children's special needs.

Mainstream curriculum with support

First of all, support means the various forms of help needed to overcome or minimize the impediment of poor attainments in reading and writing. In primary schools this often takes the form of special reading groups and, as figures already quoted show, teachers hear poor readers more frequently. The Bullock Report suggested that where additional staffing is available for remedial work this might be used to free the class teacher for working with the special reading group. This would make it more likely that the remedial work was related to the rest of a child's learning. It would also give the teacher more time to be thoroughly acquainted with the child's difficulties and needs which would be an advantage in ordinary class work. Unfortunately staffing levels are not so favourable as they were at the time of the Bullock Report. Primary schools are, of course, accustomed to organizing teaching for a wide range of ability and attainment and to that extent support is easier to give.

In secondary schools, withdrawing children for additional help is widely practised. The teaching is often based on books and materials produced for older backward readers but remedial teachers in recent years have been concerned to relate remedial work more closely to the reading and writing demands of subject teaching by the use of appropriate texts and the application of phonic work and spelling to words needed in subject teaching. A wider role for the remedial teacher has been developing as an adviser to other staff, sometimes involving assistance and co-teaching in the ordinary classroom. While all teachers could not be expected to be experts in literacy, they should at least have a basic knowledge of the reading process and, particularly, an awareness of features of reading material and the language of instruction which make for difficulty in reading and understanding.

Many children with literacy difficulties have a reasonable understanding of the content of subjects. Some others have considerable difficulty in comprehending concepts and explanations. They are likely to be judged as limited in intelligence. The word intelligence, implying an ability possessed to a certain measurable amount is not particularly helpful. It is more useful to consider the types of thinking required in different kinds of learning at different stages – and how they may be assisted and supported. Some examples are given in books by Boardman and Cowie referred to in Chap. 5. In essence, this form of support is aimed at improving mental functioning – observing, reasoning and acquiring appropriate language. At the primary stage, thinking develops which enables children to 'make sense of their experience' – of the actual – by means of practical and verbal inquiry, seeing similarities and differences, causes and effects, developing the mental operations of classifying and ordering in series. The curriculum, particularly in mathematics, environmental study and primary science, illustrates and provides the means for this growth in thinking. The slow learner is less likely to focus on the essentials of an experience (e.g. a visit, a TV programme, an activity or story). Being less ready to contribute or respond to questions they are less stimulated to develop their thinking. Difficult though it is in a class to give the slow ones *more* attention it is possible to try to ensure *equivalent* attention in these situations where they are so easily overshadowed by more verbal and lively children.

During the secondary school, thinking develops which enables the individual to go beyond the actual – to consider possibilities, to venture explanations or hypotheses and to develop abstract ideas which are increasingly required as children go through the secondary curriculum. Children need opportunity and the stimulation to think around possibilities, to consider different points of view and to attempt judgements. Though the capacity to do so may appear limited in slow learners, it is nevertheless important that they should have the experience through discussion, from hearing others attempting explanations and the stimulus provided by appropriate materials. Although they may not develop the levels of thinking and judgement required for conventional success in academic studies, they will certainly need in leavers' courses and in further education – and in life – to consider different courses of action and behaviour, different points of view. A number of approaches and materials in use in schools, referred to in Chap. 5, exemplify this and have been used successfully with the less able.

A third kind of support is a personal and emotional one. It is difficult for the normally successful person to appreciate fully the anxiety, frustration and lowered self-esteem which failure may result in. Of course, some children cope well through having compensatory achievements. Some 'cope' by opting out. Support includes the relationship through which teachers encourage and sustain pupils' hope and motivation. An equally important message is signalled by the practical steps which are taken by the teacher and through the organization of the school to help slow learners and to convey the belief that they can progress.

This aspect of support has always been an important feature of remedial teachers' work. When good progress is made, it is rarely possible to know how far progress has been due to the excellence of the teaching methods or to the change brought about in the pupils' attitudes to their tasks and to themselves as learners. Lawrence (1971) has emphasized the importance of the opportunity for low achievers to talk about themselves and their difficulties in an empathic relationship with an adult – not necessarily a teacher. He has also discussed the notion of 'locus of control' – the extent to which the individual feels that he or she can influence what happens to them; that their own efforts are important. Counselling in this sense is not the responsibility of any one person. Certain activities, subjects or particular teachers often provide situations which are conducive to conversations which help pupils to come to terms with themselves and their problems.

Related to this is the need for measures to assist the social integration of slow learners, particularly the most retarded. Some, of course, mix and relate normally with their peers but a few turn out to be those least chosen as friends or participants in groups.

Sometimes it is because they have least to offer or have personality traits which do not attract other children. Sometimes they are timid and withdrawn. Yet to feel a member of the group and to have friends is a basic requirement for settled adjustment to learning. Normal children starting school and those in their first few weeks at a new school are often tense and unsettled until they find the security of friendship or the small group. Some unfortunate children do not find this security and comfort or the stimulus of sharing talk and activity with others.

How the social participation and acceptance of children with special needs can be promoted is a question which has come very much to the fore in relation to the integration issue in recent years. One of the arguments for not separating children into special schools or classes is that they should have the benefit of mixing normally with other children. But it is being recognized that social integration may not just happen; teachers need to consider how it may be helped and promoted. Many studies have shown that the children with personal limitations may be socially rather isolated, lacking friends and participation in children's groups. Rather fewer studies have explored the practical measures which teachers can take. A first step is that the teachers should communicate equal acceptance of all pupils. Ways of pairing or grouping children for activities can be helpful and in some settings peer tutoring (an older or more capable child helping another) has been found beneficial.

It follows from all that has been said so far that support is based on an understanding of individual children's difficulties and needs. In the majority of children with mild learning difficulties understanding is achieved by teachers in the course of teaching and much emphasis has been put in recent years on teachers' records of pupils' progress and development. Where it is possible for teachers who know the child to meet and discuss their needs, it is often the case that discussion reveals new information and a different view of the difficulties, often stimulating ideas about a new approach to their learning and adjustment needs. Needless to say, communication within a school should ensure that essential information is known – a mild hearing impairment, an epileptic condition, a respiratory condition, a disturbing factor in the child's life or home situation. It is difficult to ensure communication of essential information in a large school and it may get forgotten or overlooked in a small one.

A major form of support for children with special needs is the advice and help of advisers, specialist advisory teachers and other specialists. The Warnock Committee recommended the idea of an advisory and support service as a means of deploying as effectively as possible special teaching skills and expertise in support of children with special needs wherever they are being educated. They were not suggesting a new service but closer integration of existing staff resources – special education advisers, teachers in the remedial service, visiting specialist teachers concerned with sensory and other impairments. It was envisaged that the school psychological service would remain a separate though complementary service. The first aim of support services would be direct advice to the teacher in the classroom, including help in teaching methods and resources for particular children and with assessment procedures and curriculum development. There are already examples of support service developing along these lines and with innovative methods of organization (Muncey and Ainscow, 1983).

Last but not least we should see parents as a resource. Experience has been accumulating about ways in which parents can be involved in various ways to help their children's development and education. Parents are very receptive at pre-school and infant stages and more could be done at later stages of schooling. In Chap. 6 examples are given of ways in which parents, with suitable guidance, were able to make a significant contribution to their child's progress.

Specific learning difficulties

As well as describing learning difficulties as mild, moderate or severe, the Warnock Report also referred to specific learning difficulties. The term is usually used to refer to children whose learning and performance is normal, even superior, in most ways but that there is a difficulty in particular kinds of learning. The best known are specific reading and/or spelling difficulties which occur in otherwise competent children and show some persisting effects in otherwise competent adults. There are some children who appear to have specific difficulty in mathematics which is not due to lack of effort or poor teaching. A few children and adults are weak in dealing with spatial representations in plans and diagrams and some continue to have uncertainty about orientation including left and right.

The Warnock Report's two paragraphs on the topic were mainly concerned with dyslexia. Advocates of the concept argue that there is a characteristic pattern of difficulties which are constitutional in origin, often occur in other members of the family and are not associated with low intelligence, socio-cultural deprivation and neurological deficits. Miles (1983) suggests that dyslexia is recognised from an accumulation of signs, any one of which would be of no special significance on its own. Reversing letters such as p, q, b, d, and words such as dog, was, are very common in children learning to read. Very poor spelling is another indicator and is often bizarre. Handwriting may be awkward. Other movements are often clumsy and quite commonly there are minor speech difficulties such as stumbling over the pronunciation of words. Quite often, a child has difficulty in learning to tell the time and in remembering details such as names and telephone numbers. Of course, each of these characteristics is observable in children whom no one would describe as dyslexic.

The Secretary of State's Advisory Committee on Handicapped Children considered the matter (DES, 1972, the Tizard Report; also partly reproduced in Reid, 1972). The committee acknowledged 'that it is possible to separate a minority of children with severe reading difficulty (and often spelling, writing and number problems) who fulfil some of the criteria of "specific developmental dyslexia", but we are highly sceptical of the view that a syndrome of "developmental dyslexia" with a specific underlying cause and specific symptoms has been identified.' The term 'specific reading difficulties' was proposed for the small group of children whose reading abilities are significantly below the standard they achieve in other aspects of learning.

The needs of such children require careful assessment, and teaching which seeks ways to avoid or compensate for learning processes in which there is difficulty and where this is not possible, to provide well-based methods of learning (Cotterell, 1970). It is unlikely that there is any panacea since the pattern of difficulties varies from person to person. Support in following a normal curriculum is needed with allowance being made for their poor presentation of work in class and in examinations. (Submission can be made to examining boards.) Phillips (1982) has described a student in this situation.

Dyslexia has tended to attract attention but there are other specific difficulties which should be recognized. Spelling may be very weak in spite of a reasonable level of reading. Brenner *et al.* (1967) found 3.8 per cent of 810 children surveyed had difficulties in hand-eye co-ordination, affecting writing, craftwork, copying patterns. Their weakness in school work was in spelling and mathematics but reading was often good. Children are aware of their difficulty and most accept it without too much concern although some react adversely particularly if it affects an important subject and when their weakness is attributed to not trying.

In the USA during the 1960s and 1970s, there was enthusiasm for the concept of learning disabilities and a search for an agreed definition. Definitions tend to be long but the essence of it is that learning disabilities refer to a variety of difficulties in the acquisition and use of listening, speaking, reading, writing, reasoning or mathematical abilities presumed to be due to a neurological dysfunction. An opposing point of view in the USA rejects speculation about the causes of the difficulties and regards refined assessment of psychological functions as unproductive. Attention should concentrate on the difficulties as they are manifested in learning and behaviour and how behavioural techniques and direct instruction can bring about change. It is a view which has support in the UK.

Emotional and behaviour difficulties

An assessment of the frequency, nature and sources of emotional and behaviour difficulties was an important aspect of the Isle of Wight study (Rutter *et al.*). The total population of 10- and 11-year-olds was screened by the use of parent and teacher questionnaires. Children with signs of disturbance were assessed individually for abnormalities of behaviour, emotions or relationships which were sufficiently marked or prolonged to be a handicap to the child or disturbing in the family or community. Six per cent were shown to have severe problems which were grouped as neurotic (a disproportionate degree of fears, anxiety or depression) and conduct (abnormal behaviour giving rise to social disapproval, such as fighting, bullying, delinquency). A disorder was twice as common in boys than girls. Conduct disorders were much more frequent in boys while neurotic disorders were somewhat more frequent in girls. A significant finding was that 40 per cent of children with conduct disorders showed a severe reading retardation whereas the reading attainment of the neurotic group was similar to that of a normal control group. It was suggested that both reading difficulties and anti-social behaviour may be based on similar temperamental or other characteristics in children but also, of course, that behaviour may be a maladaptive response to educational failure. An assessment of prevalence in London using the same methods and standards of assessment found that severe emotional and behaviour difficulties were twice as frequent (Rutter *et al.*, 1975).

These studies were identifying severe and persistent problems and it will be realized that many more children have lesser degrees of difficulty which affect their adjustment to school and their progress in learning or are a *reaction* to failure in learning.

The problems of some children arise partly because their basic needs for security and for consistent patterns of parenting have been inadequately met. The needs of children have been explained by Kellmer Pringle (1974) and Wedge and Prosser (1973) have summarized in *Born to Fail?* findings from the National Child Development Study which demonstrate the disadvantaged circumstances in which many children are brought up. But poor adjustment is not simply a reaction to circumstances. Some have traits of temperament or developmental difficulties which require an adaptive response from those who care for them. The right teacher at the right time and support and advice to parents at critical periods may be sufficient to bring about change.

One of the arguments for nursery school experience is that it provides an early opportunity for preventing or ameliorating adjustment difficulties. Chazan *et al.* (1980) screened the pre-school children in nurseries in two LEAs in order to identify children with special needs and to examine how such needs might be met. Of 51 children with marked needs, those with physical or sensory disabilities were easiest to cope with, those with retarded development and delayed language development presented rather more problems and some teachers were better than others at providing for them. The ones who were most difficult for teachers to cope with were the emotionally disturbed. Some were restless and disruptive – 'stubborn, self-willed, defiant; if he doesn't get his own way, he throws temper tantrums and screams and kicks'. Children who showed extreme withdrawal were just as difficult to help – one child had not said anything to the teacher for a whole year. Another would never play with other children and was very reluctant to be drawn into any group activity. The researchers considered that much more could be done to help such children and their teachers by having advice and practical guidance from educational psychologists and by working with parents.

When children enter infant school, teachers are accustomed to the variation in their independence, self-confidence and their ability to relate to others. Lesley Webb (1967) has described the difficulties of children observed over a six-year period. Of the 500 children who went through the school, 80 (16 per cent) 'presented their teachers with unusual problems of both behaviour and learning' – unusual compared with the others whose misdemeanours were of short duration and resolved by ordinary attention to their learning and social needs. The commonest expression of disturbance was aggression which accounted for 20 of the cases. Very withdrawn behaviour was the problem of nine children, severe anxiety in seven and there were small numbers for the remaining types of problem. It is worth noting that the children with special needs were spread through the families of different occupational groups – professional to unskilled. It is also worth noting that she identified a group of ten children who were noticeable for their limited language skills and lack of social and personal competencies that most children have acquired by the age of five. They were not aggressive or withdrawn or anxious but children whose deprived backgrounds (though not necessarily deprived of affection) had not prepared them for the 'culture of the school'. Though they were not difficult in behaviour, one might perceive the possibility that they might become so if they did not make progress in school learning; they might increasingly feel alienated. Lesley Webb's book shows how the infant school can do much to resolve or alleviate the problems of the one in six children whose special needs are quite considerable. In particular, she stresses co-operation with the school nurse, doctors, educational psychologists and partnership with parents. She also attaches great importance to adequate records of information about children's home circumstances, needs and the progress they make.

The majority of children with emotional and behaviour difficulties are of course in ordinary classes. Some who need help present no disciplinary problem, being withdrawn, often socially isolated, apathetic and underachieving. Some teachers are particularly good in creating an atmospherc of warmth and encouragement which enables such children to come out of their shell. Sometimes a contact with another child can be encouraged; sometimes there is a somewhat better performance or skill to be praised and nurtured. The concerned teacher usually finds some starting point for change.

When the problem is disturbing behaviour, it is more difficult because it is liable to threaten the teacher's feelings of competence and orderliness. If the teacher feels threatened, they should try to conceal it and should remember that *every* teacher has at some time had the same problem. Moreover, there is now a body of information which provides concepts and guidelines for class management and for coping with difficult behaviour. A pamphlet by Laslett (1982) outlines the nature of the teacher's task in helping a maladjusted child in ordinary classes and suggests guidelines for success in the classroom. Laslett and Smith (1984) in a short and readable book have explained the basic rules of managing a class, the place of rewards and punishments and the strategies which teachers can employ in dealing with problems. There are many expositions of behavioural methods for decreasing undesirable behaviour and for rewarding and increasing the desired behaviour (Poteet, 1973; Harrop, 1983). Redl (1952) described 17 tactics with memorable names which were derived from work with disturbed adolescents; for example, *planned ignoring* when it is better to ignore attention seeking or provocative behaviour; *hypodermic affection* when affection or praise needs to be injected; *hurdle* help when a difficulty is anticipated and early help given; *tension decontamination through humour; proximity and touch control*, etc. It is worth reading.

Whereas the approach to emotional and behavioural difficulties has tended to focus on the causes and nature of those difficulties, and more recently what the teacher can do, another emphasis has developed which views problem behaviour in relation to the school's organization and goals. The writings of Hargreaves, beginning with a study of social relations in the secondary school (1967) and others on deviance in classrooms, have drawn attention to the effects of school 'climate', expectations and organization on the occurrence of problems.

Rutter *et al.* (1979) in *Fifteen Thousand Hours* studied 12 inner-London schools and found that they differed markedly in the behaviour and attainments of pupils as judged by academic success, numbers staying on beyond 16, attendance and delinquency rates. In general, better than average schools were consistently so in terms of behaviour, attainment and delinquency rates and these effects were not due to differences in premises and administration. They stated that differences were related to their characteristics as social institutions – such factors as academic emphasis, incentives and rewards, good conditions for pupils and opportunities for responsibility. No one doubts that these are differences between schools which influence behaviour and learning and it is a useful corrective to the tendency we have had to see difficulties in adjustment and learning in terms of the pupil's disabilities and to give rather less attention to the social and organizational setting of the school.

Special provisions

During the 1970s, there was a growth of special arrangements in ordinary schools such as nurture groups aiming to give infants the social, emotional and play experiences that they needed to be able to make successfully the transition to the ordinary class. Labon (1973) described adjustment groups in primary schools as a means of helping children in a 'therapeutic' setting to develop the ability to form relationships with adults and other children and to communicate with a sympathetic adult. Special adjustment units are also set up in some secondary schools. Jones (1971; 1973) described one such unit in a comprehensive school and, importantly, the conditions which are needed to ensure that it is an integral part of the school and not 'a dumping ground' for difficult youngsters. Rodway (1981) has edited a booklet published by the Association of Workers with Maladjusted Children in which the teachers of five special classes in different parts of the country describe their methods and the approach. During the 1970s, withdrawal units sometimes termed 'sanctuaries' were set up for children with disturbed or disruptive behaviour. Rabinowitz and also Daines have written chapters on this form of provision in a book on behaviour difficulties in secondary schools (Gillham, 1981).

The first child guidance clinics were established in the 1920s and 1930s and educational psychologists were appointed to some local education authorities before 1939. It was only after the 1944 Education Act that educational provision began to be made for maladjusted children. In 1950 there were 21 residential and two day schools catering for just under 600 children. In 1982, about 10,000 pupils were receiving residential special education, about 6,000 attending day special schools and about 1,500 were attending designated special classes in ordinary schools, i.e. only a fraction of the number of children judged by surveys to have marked emotional or behaviour difficulties.

Special classes or units in ordinary schools are generally seen as short-term placements aiming at return to mainstream. Generally children so placed have less severe difficulties. The combination of a less demanding environment, a therapeutic relationship with the teacher, opportunities for success and for remedial work in attainments together with home liaison hopefully result in the child being better able to cope with the ordinary class.

The serious step of recommending residential school placement is normally only made when there are very disturbed, stressful or emotionally depriving home circumstances. Placement is seen as a means of giving disturbed children the chance for a few years of developing, personally and educationally, in a secure and therapeutic environment in which they can learn to trust adults, can express and learn to cope with their own feelings, anxieties and aggression and hopefully will be better able to cope with the environment they return to.

Day special school placement is more likely to be considered when there are positive factors in the home situation and when the child's problems are mainly related to his or her adjustment to ordinary schooling. The day school can more easily maintain helpful liaison with the child's home and neighbourhood school.

The experience of these schools has contributed much to our understanding of disturbed behaviour in children and young people, to our understanding of how teachers and other adults may helpfully respond to it and how education may be therapeutic. The experience of teachers of maladjusted children are described in books and articles listed at the end of this chapter.

List of further reading

DEVEREUX, K. (1982) *Understanding Learning Difficulties*. Milton Keynes: Open University Press.

FRASER, B. (1984). *Society, Schools and Handicap*. Stratford-upon-Avon: National Council for Special Education.

GULLIFORD, R. (1971) *Special Educational Needs*. London: Routledge and Kegan Paul.

HAIGH, G. (1977). *Teaching Slow Learners*. London: Temple Smith.

HOLT, J. (1969). *How Children Fail*. Harmondsworth: Penguin.

LEACH, D.J. and RAYBOULD, E.C. (1977). *Learning and Behaviour Difficulties*. London: Open Books.

WEBER, K. (1982). *The Teacher is the Key*. Milton Keynes: Open University Press.

WILSON, M. and EVANS, M. (1980). *Education of Disturbed Pupils*. Schools Council Working Paper 65. London: Methuen Educational.

CHAPTER 4
The Organization of Provision

Teachers are inevitably mainly concerned with the immediate problems of classes and the special help to be given to particular children but it is also important to give some thought to the overall strategy within which the individual efforts of teachers are made. It may well be that some of the problems which teachers meet could have been avoided or alleviated by earlier and better provision; the organization of provision in schools might reduce some problems or provide more positive solutions. We recognize the importance of the early identification of special needs, the continuity of special help from early childhood to late adolescence (if needed), the value of involving parents and the need for co-operation and assistance with a range of advisers and specialists from education, health and social services.

Early recognition

Learning difficulties and disabilities should be recognized as early as possible. Severe physical, sensory and mental disabilities are usually detected early in the pre-school years through regular surveillance by child health services – hospitals, clinics, the work of general practitioners and health visitors. Less severe disabilities may not be identified until later in the pre-school years and sometimes in the early school years. In particular, delayed development, retarded speech and language, and emotional and behaviour difficulties show themselves in the nursery school or class or in the pre-school play group. Where such difficulties do not respond to ordinary pre-school experience, consideration should be given to methods for providing special help including the involvement of parents and the advice and assistance of specialists such as speech therapists and educational psychologists.

There has been considerable interest in nursery education as a means of improving children's language and thinking and also in the early integration of children with special needs. Studies of pre-school groups have explored the nature of verbal interaction between children and between adults and children and the ways in which social interaction between handicapped and non-handicapped children may be promoted (Gunstone *et al.* 1982; Guralnick, 1980). Valuable as ordinary pre-school experience is for all children, there are specific interventions we can make to assist the development and adjustment of children with special needs.

Unfortunately, although the Plowden Report and the Warnock Report both made a strong case for increased provision for pre-school children, the national average for children attending nursery schools or classes is only about 22 per cent. The figure for metropolitan authorities, however, is 33 per cent and several inner city areas provide for 50 to 60 per cent. (With more children entering infant school before five, 56 per cent of four-year-olds are recorded as being in school.)

The infant school years are, however, the first at which all children come under the observation of teachers and it is also the time when there is most likely to be contact with parents. Infant teachers normally know well which children are having learning or adjustment difficulties but the case has been argued for a 'screening' procedure which looks at whole age groups in an area to identify children with difficulties in learning. For example, the Croydon Checklist consists of 19 items covering the areas of communication, perceptual-motor, emotional-social and response to learning situations. The teacher simply records Yes or No for each child to statements such as 'Draws/paints recognisable objects', 'Can persist at a task','Is the speech free from infantile substitutions?' A certain number of negative responses is taken as the 'cut-off' point indicating children who might be considered in more detail to assess their needs. The development and use of this simple procedure in Croydon was complemented, as it should be, by in-service courses for infant teachers and the preparation of appropriate teaching materials (Wolfendale and Bryans, 1980).

There are many different ways of focusing attention on the children who are not progressing. Some school psychological services have devised their own simple procedures, often in a collaboration with infant teachers which continues into workshop courses to consider methods to help children noted by the procedure. Cornwall and Spicer (1982), in a survey of the work of educational psychologists, found that a screening procedure was employed in 85 per cent of local education authorities, the most popular ages being third-year infants, first-year juniors – or third-year juniors prior to the transition to secondary schools.

A screening procedure applied to a whole age group in an area has to be economical in time, materials and staff resources. It is therefore a simple procedure or 'screen', not usually a thorough test procedure. It is not predictive of future educational achievement; it should not result in labelling children. It should aim to focus attention and additional help on children who appear to need it now. Perhaps its main benefits are the sharpening of teachers' perceptions of children who need additional help; and also the in-service training which follows.

The Bullock Committee (DES, 1975) on language and reading expressed some reservations about the use of screening tests over whole age groups since they thought the best method of screening is systematic observation and recording by teachers with selective assessment of pupils who are having difficulties. Certainly, Moses (1982) found that teachers in six infant schools had no difficulty in identifying 18 per cent of children as having special educational needs – three-quarters with learning problems and a third with emotional and behaviour difficulties. The important thing, of course, is assistance and advice in methods of assessing and providing for these needs and many school psychological services are particularly interested in work at this age level.

The DES Circular 1/83, which explained the practical implications of the 1981 Education Act, stressed that all schools should try to identify children with special needs and that there should be a progressive extension of involvement from the teacher to the headteacher, to a specialist teacher (e.g. a remedial or advisory teacher), the educational psychologist, the school doctor, nurse and other professionals in education, health and social services and the parents should be involved. Teachers should be encouraged to keep full records of their pupils' progress and to include information about professional consultations and assessments.

In other words, children who are not making progress in learning, or in their adjustment and behaviour, should be the subject of consultation within the school. If changes in teaching do not prove effective, other advice should be sought. Early recognition and appropriate remedial measures are desirable since problems often become more resistant to remedy as a result of a growing sense of failure and dislike of school work.

Special help in primary schools

Children enter school at five with varied degrees of readiness for learning, depending partly on the social, intellectual and language experience they have had at home or in nursery school or play group and partly on their general development. It is an accepted and integral part of teaching in infant or first schools to provide for the wide range of learning abilities, speech and language development, social and emotional maturity. It is a time when advice and assessment may be needed from a speech therapist, doctor, educational psychologist or an advisory teacher in the cases where sensory, physical, speech or learning problems give the school particular cause for concern. Lesley Webb (1967) has provided a very readable account of the various kinds of special need in an infant school and how the teachers worked with advisers and with parents to assist children's educational progress or their personal adjustment. In her school in a 'favourable' area and with a relaxed atmosphere and a stable staff, the percentage of children with problems ran at 16 per cent over a five-year period; she recognizes that in a 'disadvantaged' area the proportion can be as high as 50 per cent. Many of the problems are emotional and behavioural (aggression; pilfering; withdrawn or over-anxious children) and, since insecurity and unhappiness are not conducive to learning, such children are usually educationally retarded as well.

It is often difficult to determine whether a child is developmentally retarded or emotionally disturbed. One experienced infant school teacher was puzzled by a boy whose work was immature and disorganized. He was also unco-operative and stubborn. Then she began to perceive that he *did* want to relate to her; his stubbornness and sulkiness occurred very noticeably when she praised other children. If there were visitors in the room claiming her attention, he would be sure to be his most difficult and awkward. She was experienced enough to take encouragement from behaviour which a less experienced teacher might have found increasingly worrying. About the same time she began to notice that he was concentrating better, his drawings were becoming more organized and detailed and he was learning to recognize some words. His problems in adjustment were related to extreme over-protection at home and also reflected the home's hostile attitude to the world. The teacher's determination to understand and help was in this case rewarded.

This account, like the case studies in Lesley Webb's book, expresses the essence of provision for special needs at the infant school stage: observation of the children's development in a setting which gives them security, which helps them to adjust to teachers and other children and also provides them with an appropriate educational experience is a basis for assessing their needs.

For many years, it has been usual to form primary classes to include the full range of ability and attainment. A survey by HMIs (DES, 1978a) found that few schools employed streaming (only 6 per cent even in the 11-year-old age group). In nearly a quarter of the schools, the small size required a mix of ages as well but a substantial number of schools deliberately choose to have a mix of ages in classes, termed family grouping or vertical grouping. The survey also found that schools regularly grouped children by attainment for particular purposes especially mathematics, reading and writing and teachers often worked co-operatively, for example regrouping two classes at times to give special attention to slow learners. Nearly half the schools were able to organize withdrawal of groups or individuals for additional attention and just less than a fifth had help from a peripatetic remedial teacher. With such a variety of alternatives, it is not surprising that very few schools organized a special class (7 per cent at 11 years).

The Bullock Report a few years earlier also found that three-quarters of schools in their survey withdrew children for individual and group help and at that time 70 per cent of the teachers giving it were part-time teachers. Some concern was expressed that remedial work may thus not be related to the children's general learning experience and much of the benefit may be lost if the class teacher is not able to build upon the remedial teaching. This view may be considered in relation to the equivocal findings of attempts to evaluate the results of remedial teaching. Although children given remedial teaching make gains, ultimately they are often not significantly different from others not given remedial help (Chazan, 1967) and the rate of improvement may not be sustained when remedial teaching ends. The findings underline the importance of a close link between remedial work and work within the class and the need for continuing support by the class teacher. A Schools Council project made classroom observations of the teaching of reading and confirmed other findings that primary teachers do ensure that they hear poor readers regularly – often daily – but the time is often short and tends not to include specific help. The project suggested that as reading skill develops, children might be heard less often but for a longer time in order to diagnose weaknesses on which to give individuals specific teaching (Southgate *et al.*, 1981). The same need for monitoring progress applies in mathematics, spelling and handwriting.

In a number of areas, advisory services are developing check lists of basic skills development which assist this monitoring progress and ways are being explored for giving support to teachers in providing for children with special needs through in-service training, the co-ordination of remedial and support services, the work of educational psychologists and in some places by seeing special schools as a resource for other schools (Hallmark and Dessent, 1982; Muncey and Ainscow, 1983).

The co-operation and active involvement of parents should be seriously considered. They are usually aware of their children's difficulties and the majority are concerned. Some indeed will probably be trying to help the child, possibly in unproductive ways. The results of programmes in which parents have been given precise guidance on how to help their children (see p. 110) have been obtaining very promising results in terms of pupils' progress and of parent and child satisfaction. There are also more general ways in which schools have tried to help parents understand what the school is doing. For example, Wilton (1975) described a scheme whereby parents acted as mother-helpers in an infant school on a rota basis and so became more aware of what the school was doing. In some American pre-school projects, the effect of this type of parent involvement was found to benefit the development of younger children in the family when they arrived at school age.

The problem is not, of course, simply one of extra help in learning basic educational skills but of how to help slower children to participate in other areas of the curriculum. Although they may appear to have less to offer in activities or classroom discussion, it is important that they should be helped to participate and not be left out because more verbal or practically competent children readily attract notice. It is a well-tried practice in classrooms to give the quiet or unconfident children suitable responsibilities and recognition for achievements, even though small ones, and to seek to draw them into discussion of an activity or the follow up to a television programme or story. Children who have difficulty in learning usually have some things (e.g. art, puppets, physical activity) in which they are relatively more successful or in which success can be engineered. Likewise, those who are socially on the fringe of children's groups or even isolated need help to relate to and be more accepted by their peers. Feeling securely part of the class group is an essential basis for progress in learning. A very readable portrayal of the slow learner's situation is given in a Scottish Education Department booklet on children with learning difficulties (Scottish Education Department, 1978) – their gradual awareness of being different and the growth of a sense of failure.

Organization in secondary schools

At the secondary stage, the question of how to provide for pupils with learning difficulties becomes more complex because of the increasing demands on literacy, numeracy and the understanding of subject-matter and because of the increase in specialist subject teaching. The traditional method of organization has been by streaming based on measures of ability and attainment (such as group tests of verbal reasoning, reading and mathematics) together with information from primary schools.

The lowest class (or classes) have often been reduced in size and designated remedial. The improvement of literacy and numeracy was a major goal in the first year or two and it was generally considered necessary to provide an adapted curriculum taught by methods suited to their needs. Much depended on the teachers who had the main responsibility for such classes and many of those who were drawn to this work had qualities which enabled them to make a warm and supportive relationship with less successful pupils and with others whose difficulties were emotional and behavioural rather than simply in learning.

In the last decade or so, the disadvantages of streaming have been realized and a mix of other forms of organizations have become common. In the first place, early classification into streams does not sufficiently allow for possibilities for change and development in abilities and attainment and, indeed, by offering a different or reduced curriculum may increase and perpetuate differences and make it more difficult for pupils to move out into other classes. Though limited in attainments, some slow learners are not necessarily so limited in ability and some have potentialities which are not developed within a reduced curriculum. Moreover, the lowest streams may feel set apart and sense being stigmatized. They are likely to perceive themselves as unsuccessful and as not valued in the school with consequent lowering of motivation, negative self-image, and hostility towards school.

There can be no simple solution partly because the general level and range of ability, attainment and other pupil characteristics vary widely across schools; the special educational needs of children with learning difficulties are also diverse. Among the alternative methods of grouping pupils are *broad bands*, containing a wider range of ability than in streamed classes. For example, a nine form entry might be grouped into three broad ability bands each containing three parallel classes. Some departments may decide to form *sets* according to ability and attainment especially in subjects such as mathematics or science where teaching follows a sequential development of knowledge and concepts. Another alternative is to form class groups of *mixed abilities* for the first year or for two or three years. This poses the problem of mixed ability teaching so that both the able and less able are catered for but also provides the potential advantages of raising expectations and of pupils benefiting from co-operation and social interaction.

An HMI discussion paper on mixed ability work in comprehensive schools (DES, 1978b) included a section on children with special needs and concluded that, where there is good planning and differentiation in objectives, teaching materials and methods, mixed ability teaching may on balance make better provision for them. In essence, the account accepts the importance of a wider range of stimulation through teaching and discussion for pupils with a reasonable level of ability though with poor attainments – those with specific and mild learning difficulties. The report recognizes the particular difficulties of children with limited general abilities whose understanding of concepts and capacity to see relationships is liable to result in fragmented learning with few opportunities to consolidate the limited amount they may be expected to learn from a particular lesson or series of lessons.

At the same time, they rightly suggest that such children may be seriously underestimated and expectations for them may be too limited. Kerry and Sands (1982) also comment, on the basis of a three-year study of mixed ability work in 37 schools, that pupils of low ability seem often to do better than expected. 'They are able to take part in work which is pitched a bit above them and their self-confidence may increase as teachers' expectation rises.' They add, of course, that quite the opposite effect may result from impossible demands with resulting loss of confidence and deterioration in performance. The study in the Nottingham Teacher Education Project has produced some useful workbooks on mixed ability teaching (Kerry and Sands, 1982) and on teaching slow learners (Bell and Kerry, 1982).

In a further publication, Sands (1982) stresses that mixed ability teaching is an advanced teaching skill requiring a bank of techniques and procedures. Although it requires a move away from *whole class* teaching, there is still a place for it if used judiciously. Some information and some experiences (such as audio-visual presentations) are best given to the class as a whole. Preparation for an experience and a follow up afterwards are obviously needed for the whole group.

Sands makes the important distinction between individual and individualized learning. *Individualized* learning means that tasks are devised or selected to match a child's needs, abilities and attainments. *Individual* work usually consists of the same tasks for each member of the class working by themselves and at their own pace. In practice, individualization implies the selection of content, activities, concepts and reading levels in the learning materials to provide for at least the most able, the average and the least able pupils. Individualization is of course needed in the assessment of work produced and the kind of comment and help which is given.

Sands found that *group* work was seen by many teachers as an essential approach in mixed ability teaching, enabling children to learn co-operatively and from each other, accepting their individual strengths and weaknesses. It may enable the slow learners to participate in group achievement rather than suffer their own failure and, perhaps most important of all, it gives them the stimulus of interaction with more able children. The project found, however, that group work meant different things to teachers. Most frequently it was used to refer to pupils seated together but working on similar but individual tasks. Group work involving several pupils contributing to a *common* task was much less frequent. This kind of group effort is usually enjoyed by pupils and can be valuable for the slow learner.

A final mode in mixed ability teaching is *team teaching* in which a group of teachers pool their knowledge and teaching skills in teaching combined groups. Teachers with relevant experience or skills can assist the most and the least able and a suitable range of experiments and tasks may be arranged. Providing appropriate work for several levels of ability is a considerable task. The HMI report on mixed ability teaching commented that quite often a stimulating lesson was followed by a dull and sterile workcard. (Another aspect is indicated in the title of an article by Wragg, 'Death by a thousand worksheets'!) Sands and Kerry report that over the three-year period of their project, the proportion of schools employing mixed ability teaching remained the same at 27 per cent but the schools represented changed as their views of its viability rose or changed with experience.

A higher proportion of 500 schools surveyed by Reid *et al.* (1981) were found to be using mixed ability grouping: more than half in the first year though this declined to 18 per cent in the third year which was balanced by an increase in the use of streaming (9 per cent to 12 per cent) and banding (23 per cent to 32 per cent). The use of sets increased from 5 to 23 per cent.

A recent survey by Clunies-Ross and Wimhurst (1983) obtained information from 698 secondary and middle schools about the organization and staffing of provision for slow learners. Schools used four main types of provision in different combinations: separate special classes; placing children in sets in certain subjects according to ability and attainment; withdrawal of children from classes at certain times for remedial help; special options among courses for fourth and fifth years.

Separate classes for slow learners were arranged mostly in the 11 to 13 age range in order to teach them in smaller groups. In only 3 per cent of schools was it the sole form of provision. The advantages were seen as providing a stable learning environment, providing emotional security and easing the transition from primary to secondary school. In many cases, one teacher was responsible for much of the timetable. Suitable resource material and trained and experienced staff enabled individual special needs to be well catered for. Headteachers noted that the restricted curriculum created difficulties in transferring pupils back to ordinary classes and also limited the choice of options in the fourth years. They also commented on the danger of the class becoming isolated and labelled as a special group with adverse effects on pupils' self-confidence and social participation. There were also problems in re-integrating them into mainstream classes.

Slow learner sets were commonly organized for English and maths, less often for humanities, modern languages and science. Forty per cent of schools used sets in the first year and 60 per cent for the fourth and fifth years. The main advantage was considered to be that slow learners could be taught in groups of up to 20 by subject specialists, thus avoiding the restricted curriculum of a special class as well as its disadvantages of segregation and labelling. Use of sets also increased the chances of pupils joining mainstream sets in subjects where they are more capable – which is true of some low achievers.

Optional courses for slow learners were mainly fourth and fifth year courses specially designed for slow learners, sometimes taught by remedial staff but usually by subject specialists. Special options were seen as giving slow learners a similar opportunity as other pupils for choice. Some schools reported good effects of the arrangement.

Withdrawal systems. Eighty-five per cent of schools made use of withdrawal from normal teaching groups in order to give pupils individual help without segregating them. While there is the possibility of losing subject teaching time, this may be avoided to some extent by withdrawing in English or maths; sometimes the student has the choice of when to withdraw. Sometimes, too, students feel embarrassed at being singled out for withdrawal. But generally the view of teachers was that it was a preferred method, combining the stimulus of mainstream with the benefits of individual tuition.

The information obtained in this study showed a very different pattern of provision from the HMIs' survey in 1969. There has been a marked move to mixed ability grouping in the first three years of secondary schooling with various combinations of alternatives for giving special teaching to low achievers. Twenty-two per cent of schools used all four methods, 34 per cent used three of them. The remainder used one or two methods. There is probably no 'best buy' since schools with different catchment areas respond to differences in the range of ability and attainment in their intake and the frequency of learning and behaviour difficulties. The philosophy and policy of the school, the readiness of subject specialists to adapt teaching to the slow learner, the availability and deployment of remedial/special education teachers are other factors in decisions about organization.

Some of the considerations in deciding how to cater for low achievers are easily stated; only further experience and evaluation of actual practice can provide the evidence. It is an important principle that forms of provision should not unnecessarily separate pupils from their age group. It sets them apart; it may create a stigma; it may reduce their self-concept, limit socialization and may mean a reduced curriculum. On the other hand, there are pupils whose basic attainments and comprehension of curriculum content are sufficiently poor as to create difficulties for themselves and their teachers; some also find a large school confusing and feel insecure. They may appear to need a special setting but may this be denying them the opportunity to learn to cope with a normal environment? Much, of course, depends on how curriculum content and methods can be adapted to their needs and how far remedial or advisory teachers can be deployed to assist this.

The role of the remedial department

The original function and central expertise of remedial teachers is the assessment of learning difficulties and the planning and teaching of remedial programmes in basic educational skills. The way that expertise is deployed has become varied with the changes in the organization of schools and in views about how children with learning difficulties may be best helped. In 1969, only one-third of secondary schools in an HMI survey had a remedial department. Ten years later Clunies-Ross and Wimhurst found that three-quarters of schools had a remedial department ranging from small units with only one person to others with teams of up to 13 teachers.

Golby and Gulliver (1979) in a review of remedial education develop a well-stated case for redefinition of the role of the remedial/special teacher. They argue that the concept of remedial education reflected particular notions of normality and, therefore, of abnormality but that curricular and organizational changes in schools have pushed out the boundaries of what we mean by 'normal'. Teachers have increasingly accepted an obligation to tailor their material to suit children of very different abilities with the result that pupils have greater opportunity for participating in the normal curriculum. The role of the remedial teacher as a kind of 'ambulance service' is reducing. The remedial teacher should contribute to curricular and organizational change; be supportive to the pupil and subject teacher in assisting access to the curriculum; and should also have a preventive role, identifying and helping pupils before problems arise.

In the same year the National Association for Remedial Education (NARE) published guidelines which defined the functions of heads of remedial departments in five areas: the assessment and identification of children with learning difficulties, for example, by the use of tests within a screening procedure and by contact with feeder primary schools; a prescriptive role preparing and implementing individualized programmes and basic learning more widely in the school; a supportive role in relation to grouping of pupils, and advisory work in respect to remedial work across the curriculum; a liaison role with support services and parents; teaching individuals and groups including those with behaviour difficulties and co-operating with colleagues on a team teaching basis.

Clunies-Ross and Wimhurst found evidence in varying degrees of these functions in the schools studied but remarked that less than 3 per cent of schools adopted the strategy of using remedial teacher support in mainstream classes. 'While much has been written about the growth of this aspect of the remedial teacher's role, the research found little evidence of its existence.'

Ferguson and Adams (1982) gave an interesting account of what remedial teachers do when they are team teaching in a lesson with a subject teacher. The general picture that emerged was that the remedial teachers were not being involved in planning the lesson and were often at a disadvantage in view of the specialist content. Nearly all were cast in the role of teacher's aides. The writers conclude by questioning whether improving the quality of teaching for all pupils is the most effective way of providing extra help for children with learning difficulties.

A more influential role is indicated by Lewis (1984) through the development of an objectives-based curriculum paralleling wherever possible that of the mainstream English and mathematics departments; and also the designation of remedial/support teacher with responsibility in a particular subject department and/or year group.

The idea of closer co-operation and working between subject teachers and remedial teachers is a sound one. NARE has already effected links with subject teaching associations which will facilitate communication and mutual understanding. One of the benefits one can foresee is that remedial spelling, reading and mathematics will become less separate 'subjects' and more what they are – skills which give access to knowledge and experience.

These extended roles are unlikely to develop if the remedial teacher is mainly involved in teaching separate classes for children with the greatest difficulties in learning or if they have a big commitment to withdrawal teaching. Clunies-Ross and Wimhurst did find, however, that in schools where support in the classroom was taking place, all used withdrawal as part of the system of provision and, as a result, a tradition of informal liaison between remedial and subject teachers already existed. They also suggested that the title of the special department may be significant. A 'head of remedial' was expected by both staff and students to be responsible for the less able pupils. If they were called 'learning adviser', it was easier to work in co-operation with subject teachers and a wider range of students. Co-operation and especially co-teaching involving a subject specialist and a 'learning adviser' or advisory teacher is not as simple and straightforward as it seems.

The role of the remedial department and the remedial teacher is evolving. In the 1969 survey (DES, 1971) only 51 out of 158 schools had a special department, variously called remedial, progress or special. In the Clunies-Ross and Wimhurst (1983) survey, 76 per cent of schools had a remedial department, three-quarters of which were simply called remedial. There must be some significance in the fact that another 13 per cent of departments were called one of the following: Compensatory Studies, Special Education, Basic Studies, General Studies, Combined Studies or Integrated Studies, and that the remaining departments were called Progress, Opportunity, Learning Difficulties Department, Coaching Department, the Department of Special Educational Resources and the Individual Learning Unit. Other names included the Literacy and Numeracy Department, the Department of Special Needs, the Help Centre and the Tutorial Centre. In one school the department was named after a past member of staff and in another after the teaching block in which the suite of rooms was located. We must surely be in danger of running out of euphemisms!

The resource room

A possible alternative are the terms resource teacher and resource room which appear to be generally used in the USA (Wiederholt *et al.*, 1978; Hawisher and Calhoun, 1978). The resource room concept developed rapidly in the drive to mainstream handicapped and learning disabled children rather than providing for them in self-contained special classes, previously the main form of special educational provision. The resource teacher may be concerned with one type of handicap or with several or more generally concerned with children with special needs. The resource teacher's role includes advisory and consultative work with classroom teachers in respect of the assessment and programming of children with special needs and generally has responsibility for integrating and implementing the individualized educational programme. The pupil may be full-time in the ordinary class, or withdrawn for an hour of tuition in the resource room or may spend half a day there. Some children are mainly based in the special class but spend some period in the ordinary class unless too severely handicapped or retarded to do so. The aim is to educate the children in 'the least restrictive environment' which means educating them as close to mainstream on the continuum of alternative placements as their handicaps and needs allow. The resource teacher is an important agent in achieving this.

A similar concept and practice has been developing in Britain. Garnett (1976) described the development of her role. Initially she was responsible for a special unit for pupils with moderate learning difficulties. Unfortunately the unit was accommodated in the grounds of a comprehensive school which did not lead to much integration except for mealtimes, assemblies and some creative and practical subjects. The pupils were rejected by mainstream pupils and sometimes teased. After a year, the opportunity came to move the unit into a central position in the main school. Pupils were integrated for much of the timetable returning to the unit for mathematics and English but increasingly felt part of mainstream. Moving to another comprehensive school, Garnett (1983) was able to develop a role as a 'co-ordinator' which seems to have been similar to the American resource room/teacher model and included (a) the identification, in co-operation with senior staff, of pupils with special needs; (b) management of a resource base for meeting special needs, not only in terms of a stock of resources but providing individual tutoring for those with learning difficulties and also being a temporary haven for unsettled or disturbed pupils; (c) support and advice to mainstream teachers, in co-operation with 'key' teachers nominated in each department, with the aim of making the curriculum accessible to those with special needs.

Jones evaluated the development of a resource approach in a comprehensive school and Jones and Berrick (1980) have given an account of it. The resources department was accommodated in purpose built premises consisting of two teaching classrooms, each able to take ten pupils, a reception area, a smaller room for tutorial work or for use by visiting specialists such as the speech therapist, educational psychologist; an art/craft room; a modified kitchen for the physically handicapped; a bathroom and restroom.

The 25 to 30 children catered for included those with severe or minor physical disorders, learning difficulties, emotional and behaviour difficulties. The three teachers (a) undertook individual tuition of pupils withdrawn from regular classes; (b) accompanied a child into a subject class to give them assistance; (c) provided appropriate work or materials in consultation with the subject teacher; (d) acted as advisers in respect of particular children causing teachers concern; (e) participated jointly with form/subject teachers in liaising with parents; (f) evaluated children's progress and monitored the integration process.

Another view of the resource approach is given by Gordon (1983). He suggests that a basic requirement is a well-equipped, spacious learning and teaching area, staffed at all times by at least one resource teacher. Some pupils will spend very little time each week in the resource area and perhaps only for a few weeks. Others will initially spend a major part of their time with the resource teacher, gradually reducing. He stresses that the amount of support individual children receive should reflect a careful appraisal of their needs in which continuous monitoring of progress and adjustment in ordinary classrooms by all teachers would be important. He makes an important point that withdrawal for resource-based help should require the agreement of the pupil after the purpose of withdrawal teaching has been fully explained. He quotes a relevant sentence from Circular 1/83 which was issued to explain the Education Act 1981: 'the feelings and perceptions of the child concerned should be taken into account, and the concept of partnership should, wherever possible, be extended to older children and young persons'. A pupil's full involvement in the special help implies their involvement in the decision to receive it. A final important point is that the resource area and its teachers should really be seen to be serving the whole school. While it is difficult to avoid such a facility becoming associated with failures, difficulties and problems, Gordon is optimistic that the wider role of resource teachers and the greater range of pupils they assist (e.g. O and A level candidates with spelling and handwriting problems) should in time dispel stereotyped attitudes.

A final example of a resource approach has been described by Sayer (1983b), then the headmaster of Banbury School. As in the case of Garnett's account, the starting point was partly a special unit for 'educationally subnormal' children within the school. It was realized from assessment of the first-year intake to the school that three times as many entrants were of low ability and attainment as were officially ascertained and placed in the special department. This department and the remedial department were therefore combined into a new department catering for all special needs as a resource for the whole school. In addition, the secondary school and its feeder primary schools became a sector within which resources for identifying and providing for children with special needs became 'a continuum of response across primary and secondary schooling' which was built into the job description of teachers and other professionals working together. A similar approach across secondary schools and their feeder primary schools is being developed in Grampion Region, Scotland (Booth and Potts, 1983).

Special schools for moderate learning difficulties

The provision of special school places for 'educationally subnormal' children grew from 15,000 in 1950 to 51,000 in 1970 and the numbers increased to 57,000 by 1982 with 8,200 in designated special classes, less than 1 per cent of the school population. The increased provision over that period was a response to the previous lack of provision and to the requirements of the 1944 Education Act in respect of special educational treatment. It could also be said to have been necessary since arrangements in ordinary schools were inadequate. The developments which have been described on previous pages indicate a variety of ways of organizing provision which should lead to the Warnock concept of a continuum of alternative forms of special provision, mostly in ordinary schools but, as anticipated by the Warnock Report, special schools continuing to be needed for some children with severe and complex difficulties. There are also possibilities for new functions for the special schools as resource centres supporting and liaising with ordinary schools.

The number of children at different ages in special schools for moderate difficulties indicates something of the role of the special school. In 1982, there were nearly 600 children below the age of five. These are likely to have been children with several difficulties, for example, delayed speech and language, a low level of mental functioning, behavioural or emotional difficulties, perhaps a physical or sensory disability. A nursery class permits an early start on their education and continuing observation of their development and difficulties. Some at five will transfer to other special schools – for children with severe learning difficulties or for physical and sensory difficulties. Children with slow development which is not complicated by other problems should of course be in ordinary pre-school provision where they may receive special attention suited to those needs.

There were over 2,000 seven-year-olds, over 6,000 11-year-olds and over 7,000 15-year-olds. The primary age group is thus the period when most children are placed, although some admissions continue at the secondary stage. If a special school is seen as being needed for children (such as those referred to in Chap. 3) who have a number of difficulties in speech and language and/or motor co-ordination, very retarded attainments and perhaps also adjustment difficulties, it might be thought that their need should be recognized early with a view to transfer later to the ordinary school. Of course, teachers hope and expect that the child will respond to teaching and only refer when progress is not apparent. Sometimes, too, the child's adjustment worsens as a result of failure and the demands of the curriculum which also accounts for referrals at secondary ages.

In some areas, attempts are being made to place children early in the special school with a view to intensive help and transfer back to ordinary school – it assumes, of course, appropriate provision in ordinary schools. There is little published information about transfers from special to ordinary schools. Fleeman (1984) followed up 33 pupils who had been placed in special schools at an average of eight years and had returned to ordinary schools at an average age of 13. She found that only about 1 per cent of children in the three schools studied were transferred over a six-year period. The transfers had proved successful in 20 per cent of the cases, the children having adjusted socially quite well and even took some CSE courses. It was reasonably successful in 50 per cent though they were not all benefiting fully from the curriculum and some had adjustment difficulties. Thirty per cent were judged not to have been successful owing to a variety of problems. Of course, much will depend upon the system of provision for special teaching and individual care in the receiving schools. As these develop in the ways which have been discussed earlier, the possibilities of transfers to and from the special school should increase.

A resource centre role for the special school was suggested in the Warnock Report: that some might develop as centres of specialist expertise and of research in special education, involved in curriculum development and in-service education for teachers. Some special schools already perform some of these roles. Advisory teachers concerned with particular disabilities are often based in a special school; some schools are active in in-service education. Hallmark and Dessent (1982) described a scheme which has been running since the mid 1970s whereby certain teachers from the special school visit particular primary schools on a regular basis to help teachers organize programmes for individual children nominated by the teacher. The methods adopted were derived from a programme called Portage, named after the town in the USA where it was developed. It provided a service in a rural area for parents of mentally handicapped children. The teacher visits the home once each week. The child is assessed on a developmental schedule so that two or three tasks are decided as targets for the mother to teach. The teacher demonstrates a method of training the particular skill and how to reward the learning. The following week the teacher checks the learning and, in co-operation with the parents, decides on new targets for the next week. An important feature is that sequences of behaviour are itemized in the Portage materials with suggestions of how they might be taught. It has proved a successful means of involving parents in teaching their handicapped child and has been widely used in this country (Cameron, 1982).

Hallmark and Dessent's approach involved the class teachers in primary schools in a similar way. The special school teacher helped to assess the slow learner's needs and to define specific teaching for the coming week. They were assisted in doing this by the fact that the special school had recently developed its own curriculum and prepared teaching materials which were made available to the teachers in the ordinary school. The approach may be contrasted with advisory help which is general in nature and not necessarily followed up regularly. Appropriate procedures and materials were prescribed for teaching towards specific objectives and were re-assessed each week. The authors report that, as a result, children who might have been referred to the special school were able to continue successfully in the primary school. Moreover, the primary teachers developed their skills and it became possible to transfer some children from the special to the ordinary school.

Where special schools are close to an ordinary school, perhaps on the same campus, this co-operation is facilitated but perhaps as important as location is the readiness of both ordinary and special schools to work together in this and other ways. The special school has expertise in teaching children who have considerable learning problems; the ordinary school has pupils with similar even if slightly less difficulty. The ordinary school may be able to reciprocate in other ways – for example, a small special school may not have teaching expertise in certain curriculum areas. There is also the benefit of at least social interaction between pupils and some pupils might become partially integrated in the ordinary school.

List of further reading

BELL, P. and KERRY, T. (1982). *Teaching Slow Learners in Mixed Ability Classes* (a self-instructional handbook of strategies and suggestions for teaching). Basingstoke: Macmillan Educational.

BOOTH, T. and POTTS, P. (Eds) (1983). *Integrating Special Education*. Oxford: Blackwell.

HODGSON, A., CLUNIES-ROSS, L. and HEGARTY, S. (1984). *Learning Together*. Windsor: NFER-NELSON.

MCCALL, C. (1983). *Classroom Grouping for Special Need*. Stratford-upon-Avon: National Council for Special Education.

CHAPTER 5
Curricular Needs

Curriculum change

For some time now, the school curriculum has been the subject of inquiry and debate as schools responded to changes in society and the organization of schooling. In the 1960s the move towards reorganization on comprehensive school lines, the preparations for raising the school leaving age to 16 (which took place in 1972) and the funding of curriculum development projects by the Schools Council, the Nuffield Foundation and by some local education authorities all stimulated curriculum thinking and experiment. In the 1970s a gradual increase in the use of mixed ability grouping in secondary schools – long established in primary schools – posed the problems of formulating and teaching a common curriculum for the wide range of ability and attainment. In recent years, the DES has also shown a close concern for balance and breadth in the curriculum and has issued a number of discussion documents as well as accounts of surveys of practice in schools.

Curriculum for special needs

The curriculum for children with special needs has the same aims as for other children. The Warnock Report expressed these eloquently: 'We hold that education has certain long term goals, that it has a general point or purpose which can be definitely though generally stated. The goals are twofold, different from each other but by no means incompatible. They are first to enlarge a child's knowledge, experience and imaginative understanding and thus his awareness of moral values and capacity for enjoyment; and secondly to enable him to enter the world after formal education is over as an active participant in society and a responsible contributor to it, capable of achieving as much independence as possible.' In a similar vein, *A Framework for the Curriculum* (DES, 1980) suggested the following aims for all pupils as a basis for discussion:

(i)   to help pupils to develop lively, enquiring minds, the ability to question and argue rationally and to apply themselves to tasks, and physical skills;

(ii) to help pupils to acquire knowledge and skills relevant to adult life and employment in a fast changing world;

(iii) to help pupils to use language and number effectively;

(iv) to instil respect for religious and moral values, and tolerance of other races, religions, and ways of life;

(v)   to help pupils to understand the world in which they live, and the inter-dependence of individuals, groups and nations;

(vi) to help pupils to appreciate human achievements and aspirations.

Such statements tend to appear idealistic in the context of classroom realities with pupils who have personal and environmental disadvantages as well as reading and language levels which limit their access to the curriculum. But the statements are a reminder that as well as helping low achievers 'to use language and number effectively' which has always seemed a first priority and as well as promoting 'knowledge and skills for adult life and employment' which is readily seen as another, their education must be concerned with improving their mental and physical skills, developing a view of themselves as persons in relation to others and to society in general. They need to understand themselves and the world in which they live. They will not achieve that on a diet of books for backward readers.

The Warnock Committee commented in its chapter on curricular considerations that they were impressed by the concern shown for individual pupils with special educational needs but that they also 'became aware that the quality of the education offered them is in some respects less satisfactory. In particular, it is sometimes limited in scope and in the challenge which it presents to individuals.' It is easy to appreciate why the curriculum might sometimes be limited in scope and challenge. Difficulties in reading and writing are an impediment to children's participation in the full range of the curriculum; limitations in understanding and language are a further disadvantage for some. Moreover the methods of organizing special educational provision has often resulted in a narrowed range of subjects and limited exposure to specialist subject teachers.

Some disquiet had in fact been expressed in previous DES reports. In 1969 a survey by HMIs of work with slow learners in 28 comprehensive and 130 secondary modern schools (DES, 1971) found that 'uncertainty of aims, objectives and methods was immediately apparent in many – indeed in the majority of the schools visited. Indeed the commonly used term "remedial" may itself be indicative of a fundamental confusion.' The confusion referred to was the implication in the word 'remedial' that backwardness would be remedied by additional teaching in basic subjects whereas a suitably devised curriculum providing opportunities for growth and fulfilment would be more appropriate.

A few years later, the Bullock Report (DES, 1975) expressed a similar concern: 'Remedial help in learning to read should wherever possible be closely related to the rest of a child's learning. Children who are in need of special help sometimes have their weaknesses exposed by the very efforts designed to remedy them, particularly if these result in fewer opportunities to achieve success in other activities, such as art, crafts, drama, and music. This can be particularly true of older children for whom a monotonous and prolonged emphasis on remedial work in the basic skills occupies a major part of the time. Where this is at the expense of other parts of the curriculum which may offer them greater chances of success, the policy can be self-defeating.'

Significantly, the Bullock Report also emphasized that 'there is no mystique about remedial education, nor are its methods intrinsically different from those employed by teachers anywhere. The essence of remedial work is that the teacher is able to give additional time and resources to adapting these methods to the individual child's needs and difficulties.' The understandable tendency of remedial teachers to emphasize low achievers' special requirements and their own remedial expertise was matched by an equally understandable tendency in other teachers to perceive these children as needing specialist skills and knowledge that they did not have. Interestingly enough, this possibility was predicted by some wise man in the Board of Education in 1937 when the idea of a 'remedial teacher' was only embryonic and there were very few of them. It was suggested in a report on the education of backward children that the creation of a new class of specialist teachers 'would be as likely to hinder as to help the spread of knowledge and skill in handling backward children because of the temptation that would beset the teachers to depend on such outside help rather than upon their own resources' (Board of Education, 1937).

A similar point was made by a former Inspector of Special Education in the report of a seminar on the curriculum in special schools (Wilson, 1981). She suggested that those concerned with special education (whether in special schools or classes) felt obliged to emphasize the special character of the work and that it is 'so adapted to meet the needs of the pupils as to be conspicuously different from that of ordinary schools.' It is true that teachers in special education have tended to emphasize – or be conscious of – the special character of the work, justifiably so in respect of special *methods of teaching* such as those required for children with sensory disabilities, communication disorders and retarded development. It is less clear that the *curriculum* should be special since all children should have the opportunities which the general curriculum provides for personal growth, for understanding the environment and for preparing for living in society. Wilson in fact concludes that considerable overlap between the curricula of special and ordinary schools is possible and that there is no reason why the majority of children should not have access to four broad areas:

1. The basic skills of language and mathematics.
2. The study of people, their relationships and achievements, both in the present and at other times and places.

3. A study of both biological and physical aspects of the environment, how people are affected by the environment and how in turn they use it.
4. Practical activity, imaginative experience and creative expression.

It is not difficult to accept these four areas as desirable in the education of all children including those with special needs. There is less certainty about how teaching methods and content need to be adapted and how access to the curriculum can be effected especially when children with moderate learning difficulties are placed part-time or full-time in special schools or classes. It has tended to be regarded as separate and different provision; in the situation following the 1981 Act we are obliged to try to minimize the separateness of provision and the difference in curriculum access.

Curriculum in special schools and units

The placement of children with moderate learning difficulties in special schools has generally been perceived as necessary in order that teaching may be suited to their slower pace of learning, can provide for consolidation of basic educational skills, and other curriculum experience can be presented in a suitable way. This view has sometimes been reflected in low expectations and a diluted version of the mainstream curriculum. A Scottish Education Department survey (1981) of the curriculum for secondary children with moderate learning difficulties in special classes or schools refers to a lack of breadth, a disproportionate amount of time being given over to formal reading and a routine of computational exercises. The social subjects, art and music had a small place in the curriculum mainly because the majority of class teachers believed that their principal task was 'to get their pupils to master the skills in which their deficiencies are probably most detectable.' The report goes on to argue that basic skills practised in isolation from realistic contexts are not likely to transfer to everyday life. A broader curriculum provides the motivation for pupils to go on developing skills and also offers a range of experiences which pupils are entitled to share with their contemporaries as a means of development and fulfilment.

In some parts of the country, especially in rural areas, special units or classes cater for children with moderate learning difficulties. For example, in Wales in 1980 there were 9,000 children recorded as having learning difficulties of whom 2,377 were placed in special units or schools, 4,548 in special classes and 1,950 in ordinary classes. Whether a special class or unit can provide a balanced curriculum depends on how far other teachers are willing and able to participate in teaching the curriculum either by being timetabled in the special class at certain times or by accepting children who are ready for some partial integration in ordinary classes. Unless there is an explicit policy about this, the special class may operate in curricular isolation. Although some children may have personal and developmental needs that would make a degree of integration unwise and inappropriate, others could benefit from a wider experience especially as children in units or classes may return to mainstream with support at secondary school.

In one of the few studies of special unit provision for primary children with moderate learning difficulties, Lowden (1984) visited 72 schools in Wales. More than 90 per cent of headteachers and special unit teachers thought that some degree of integration of these children into ordinary classes was desirable but only three-quarters of the class teachers. More than half the teachers expressed a preference *not* to have slow learners in their classes. In a study of six units in secondary schools, which catered for a range of special needs, Bailey, J. (1982) found that, although the majority of teachers felt that having a special unit was a bonus for the school, there were nevertheless many practical difficulties in arranging for children from the unit to be timetabled for subjects in ordinary classes. That there should be difficulties and that some teachers are not keen to accept a pupil for part-time integration is hardly surprising since the idea has only recently come to the fore. 'Know-how' has to be built up through experience both on the part of class teachers and of teachers with a responsibility for children with special needs. It is also necessary to define what is meant by 'benefiting' from the mainstream curriculum – the class teacher and the special education teacher may have different conceptions and expectations, a point which will be considered later.

It is not really possible to generalize about the curriculum in special schools and classes since schools are so varied. They have individual characteristics; their freedom from mainstream constraints has often led to innovative approaches. It would be fair to say, however, that the emphasis has been on what is special about the curriculum rather than its correspondence with the normal curriculum on which children had failed to make progress. Special has been interpreted in various ways at different times.

One kind of emphasis derives from teachers' concern to develop knowledge, skills and personal qualities which will assist pupils' adjustment in their lives after leaving school. Many writers have referred to the goals of personal, social and vocational adequacy. An example of a curriculum which made pupils' future needs the main basis was the Illinois Curriculum Guide (Goldstein and Seigle, 1958). This was planned in terms of ten Life Functions – Citizenship, Communicating, Home and family, Leisure, Management of materials and money, Occupational adequacy, Health, Safety, Social adjustment, Travel. The plan suggests appropriate work in language, number, creative and practical activities for each area at primary, intermediate and senior levels. That kind of curriculum emphasis – a reaction against an academic one – no longer looks special, having been increasingly assimilated into the curriculum of ordinary schools and further education colleges. It is also questionable whether the curriculum for younger children should be too influenced by post-school needs. The needs arising from their age and stages of development are important considerations.

One view about how to decide priorities within the curriculum was suggested by Brennan (1974). He referred to the fact that the need for much attention to the learning of literacy and numeracy can lead to work which is 'arid, repetitive, lacking in excitement and transfer outside the school situation'. He suggested that in trying to offer a balanced curriculum adapted to their needs a distinction could be helpful between learning required to the level of *mastery or thoroughness* and learning to the level of *familiarity or awareness*. In every area of the curriculum, some skills, concepts and knowledge are important enough to require thorough learning. Certain ideas about health, safety, social and environmental knowledge might be regarded as essential, for example. There are other ideas and experience of which pupils should have awareness, even though they may not have complete understanding, so that the pupils can relate to them when they subsequently encounter them in social and other situations. He insists that learning for awareness is no less important than learning for mastery and that there should be an interaction between the two. The distinction should not be taken as implying limited expectations but rather as seeking *appropriate* expectations. We do not expect slow learners to become historians or scientists but we should aspire to give every child some sense of the past and its evidence in the contemporary environment and its events, and also some sense of the scientific and its pervasive influence on our lives and society. These are different but not limited expectations for children – and for those who teach them.

A different orientation emerged in the 1960s at a time when human abilities were being seen as less immutable and more open to the effects of training and teaching. There was considerable interest in the idea that the perceptual, motor and psycholinguistic difficulties associated with disabilities in learning could be identified by specific tests designed for the purpose and that programmes to train or remedy the weak functions could be prescribed. Thus, weaknesses in visual or auditory discrimination or in perceptual–motor tasks (such as drawing and manipulative tasks) could be remedied by training. This optimistic approach influenced remedial teaching and the planning of programmes with young children whose development was retarded. Evaluations of specific training programmes have been rather inconclusive and the validity of some of the tests (i.e. whether they were really testing specific functions) has been questioned by some of the evidence; the training may have improved specific functions but the effects were not necessarily transferred to learning school tasks. The current view is that it is both more sensible and effective to examine the actual skills to be learnt and the sequence in which they are acquired. Where necessary, particular skills can be analysed into smaller steps in the sequence, for example, the writing movements which are common to certain letter groups; perceiving the auditory similarities in certain groups of words as a preparation for phonic work. This does not mean that the teacher can be unobservant of children's particular difficulties. On the contrary, observation often provides awareness of the need for special care in planning the learning and giving practice.

It is easy to appreciate why teachers of children with learning difficulties should be receptive to approaches and methods which appear to offer new solutions. Such approaches usually contribute to understanding and to the repertoire of teaching skills but it has been increasingly recognized that the central concern should be the curriculum: what learning and experience is needed to further children's development? what skills and knowledge do they need to function successfully as members of society? how can the whole curriculum of the school contribute to the educational goals?

Like ordinary schools, special schools have engaged in curriculum development, attempting to define the school's aims, the goals for different age levels and curriculum areas and to establish teaching objectives. It is a difficult and time-consuming task which makes explicit the intentions of the school and awareness of how learning of different kinds reinforce and complement each other. Teachers derive a clearer conception of their task; new teachers can more readily perceive their role; parents and others outside the school can be given a clearer picture of what the school is trying to do.

In some areas of the curriculum, the steps towards competence in particular skills can be clearly defined and a behavioural objectives approach has been advocated. The objectives are stated unambiguously in terms of the behaviour or performance which demonstrates that learning has been achieved; the conditions or criteria for successful performance are also specified. Where the gap between one objective and the next is too great the task may be analysed into smaller steps and a variety of methods can be drawn upon for assisting the learning. Among the benefits are that the sequence of objectives and the clearly stated definition of successful performance provide the teacher with a means for frequent and regular assessment of the effectiveness of teaching and the learner with the reinforcement of success. Ainscow and Tweddle (1979) developed a curriculum in a special school in which they distinguished between the 'closed' and the 'open' curriculum. The closed curriculum consists of subjects requiring the learning of skills to a level of mastery, where learning is sequential and the objectives can be stated in terms of the required behaviour. The areas considered appropriate for this were: arithmetic, gross motor development, handwriting, language, early reading, spelling and social competence. The construction and implementation of an objectives-based curriculum is a considerable undertaking but teachers find that it gives them a structure through which they are clear about their goals and also about how individuals are progressing. Moreover, the objectives do not necessarily limit teachers' choice of methods of teaching. The methodology of this kind of approach does, in fact, provide a range of strategies which teachers also find helpful. There is, however, the question how far even in certain areas of the closed curriculum the definition of teaching objectives in behavioural terms is adequate. It is clearly appropriate in teaching motor and social competence skills but less so as a framework for teaching language and reading. Numerous articles explain curriculum planning using a behavioural objectives approach (e.g. Burman *et al.*, 1983; Cameron, 1981).

The teaching of reading, writing and number have always been regarded as priorities in the education of children with moderate learning difficulties. In recent times, language and communication have been accorded similar status. There are many reasons for this. It is obviously important that children should be able to communicate effectively, both in comprehension and expression, both in learning situations and in everyday contacts with others. Furthermore, language has been seen as a prime target in attempts to improve educational potential and performance, especially from the period of enthusiasm in the USA (reflected in the UK) for programmes of compensatory education such as Headstart which set out to alleviate the effects of social and educational disadvantage. A number of language programmes were developed, some designed to stimulate oral language and mental activity in supplementary periods of group work, others offering a highly structured programme to develop language as a tool for conceptual thinking; yet others aimed to help teachers become more aware of the nature of the language interactions between children and with teachers in the course of pre-school play or primary activities within the curriculum. There is no doubt children respond well to group language sessions and teachers report favourably about the use of highly structured programmes.

Whether or not some group work with the most language retarded is possible, the *curriculum as a whole* is the basis for a language programme, and one moreover which provides broad scope for the range of uses of language. Halliday (1969) referred to seven functions or models of language: the *instrumental* model is the language to get things done, for example, when the child wants something; the *regulatory* model, the language whereby others exercise control over him and he can control others, e.g. siblings, playmates. The *interactional* is the language of interaction between the self and others, both adults and other children. The *personal* model refers to awareness of self, as a person who can do, choose, talk, etc. The *heuristic* model is the use of language to find out about the environment, for example by questions and answers. The *imaginative* is reflected in such words as story, make up, pretend, imagine and also manifest in poems, rhymes, riddles. The *representational* model includes the means of communicating about things, expressing propositions about things in the real world. It is the function which is most evident in teaching concepts and information.

Teachers of younger children will have little difficulty in relating these models of language to children whose communication is retarded on entry to school. Some cannot make their wants known in words, some do not respond to the language of control or can only attempt to control others by physical rather then verbal means. The verbal means of making a friendship or joint play activity with another child may be insufficient, and insufficient also for firming a relationship between child and teacher. Other less retarded children may be poor at explaining how they feel, in conversing and asking questions, and in the imaginative functions of language. Often we try to develop the conceptual and representational aspect of language on a narrow base of awareness and use of language.

Whereas Halliday refers to 'relevant models of language' of which children are intuitively aware, Joan Tough (1977) has conducted studies over a long period into the uses of language by young children. By means of sound and video recording of children talking as they play, she has been able to relate children's talk to their purposes and has developed a system of classification which the many teachers who have attended her courses appear to have found useful and meaningful. First she identifies the *relationship* between the children in which the language use ranges from self-assertion to mutual recognition and concern. The other categories refer to content: *self* maintaining (identification of self-interest, justification, setting a condition, surveying alternative possibilities).

The *directive function* – monitoring individual or collaborative actions and forward planning.
The *interpretive function* –identification of something; analysing sequences, relationships and causes; the abstraction of meaning.
The *projective functions* which go beyond the immediate present:
   (i)   *predictive* functions: consider alternatives, hypotheses, anticipate consequences, predict solutions;
   (ii) *imaginative*: an object represents something or the language is purely imaginary;
   (iii) *empathic*: where the child projects himself into the feelings and life of others.
One of the potential values of a classification such as this is that it helps the teacher to observe children's play and language and can then consider what might be done to stimulate activity and related speech. It might suggest some additional play material to provoke co-operative play; alteration to the spaces in the play area; arranging for a different partner or group in the hope of stimulating a particular type of play or language function. We have rather tended to assume that providing the opportunity for activity and social interaction in young children is sufficient in itself but a number of studies have explored ways in which a child with retarded language or play can be helped to participate in co-operative play with a non-retarded child (Guralnick, 1978).

For language work at the secondary level, Halliday's 'models of language' found practical expression in language materials prepared in a project which was initiated by Halliday and carried through by Doughty *et al.* (1971). It consisted of 110 units each providing an outline for a sequence of lessons related to a particular way in which we use language. The units aimed to develop in pupils and students awareness of what language is, how it is used and to extend their competence in using language. One part was concerned with the use and nature of language, e.g. conveying information, using language expressively. The theme of a second part was language and individual man – language in relation to reality, culture and experience. A third part was concerned with language in individual and social relationships. While most of the language activities proposed could be used with less competent pupils, suggestions are made of units which are particularly suitable. For example, four adjacent units are concerned with (i) interviews on television, (ii) talking on the telephone, (iii) taking messages, (iv) being interviewed. Francis and Phillips-Johnson (1983) report very positively about trials with the materials in schools and express surprise that so few teachers knew of them.

More recently there has been considerable interest in the Instrumental Enrichment programme (Feuerstein, 1980) which consists of structured materials through which pupils learn to perceive pattern, to see relationships and to categorize, to contrast and to compare objects, events and ideas in a setting where the teacher *mediates learning through dialogue and discussion*. It aims to break through the cycle of failure, poor motivation and negative attitudes of the retarded learner. Trials have been conducted in five local education authorities in England (Weller and Craft, 1983). An evaluation of the programme and the results published so far has been made by Bradley (1983) who concludes that the results are modest and the findings inconclusive. As further experience is gained, we may anticipate the intention of 'mediating learning through dialogue' being realized within the curriculum – as indeed many teachers would claim to have tried to do.

It is generally accepted that the teaching of language and mathematics needs to be well-organized and monitored whether the necessary structure for teaching is based on a scheme of behavioural objectives or more conventional schemes for developing educational skills. It is equally important that there should be some principles to give coherence and structure for other aspects of the curriculum through which children develop in understanding and awareness, in language and communication, in their personal qualities and social adjustment. Even if they do not get as far as we would hope in literacy and numeracy – and some do not – we should be able to feel that we have educated them as people better able to cope with the situations they meet in life. An article by Atkinson (1984) provides a fascinating account of the adjustment and progress of men in mid-life who had left a special school 30 years earlier with limited basic attainments. The attainments of many had improved but, perhaps more important, most of them had learned from the experience of living and working. In providing a curriculum experience for pupils with learning difficulties, we have to consider how in school we can offer a good base for that future development. The four areas suggested by Wilson (p. 80) is a useful general statement and a

Scottish Education Department report (1981) suggests another: language and mathematical studies; social and environmental studies; practical and other skills for living; recreative and expressive activities. The curriculum implications of such statements need to be considered in relation to the ages of children and the stages of education.

Primary curricular needs

At the primary stage, whether in special or ordinary classes, the language experience, environmental study, physical and creative activities are no less important than learning reading and mathematics even though the schemes are less structured and easy to define. They provide a medium for language development and for many practical and thinking skills in which children with learning difficulties often have much need to make progress. For example, topics on people who help us, living things, materials, foods, transport, are common themes in what Wilson referred to as 'the study of people' and 'the study of the biological and physical aspects of the environment'. The problem is how to ensure that the slower children are participating sufficiently to benefit in language and understanding. It would be easy to rest content that they 'get something' from the experiences but the experienced teacher is likely to look for – and try to stimulate – communication, observation and questioning from the less responsive child. A list of objectives appropriate to different levels of observation, thinking and language used in primary science (Ennever, 1972) has relevance for other primary activities. The HMI primary school survey indicates that schools are less clear how such themes and topics might develop in later age groups with more attention to historical, geographical and scientific content. There are many concepts and words relating to time, the past, plans and maps, people, places, things and events which even though not thoroughly understood, are as much a preparation for the secondary curriculum as are basic skills.

The common curriculum in secondary schools

The surveys referred to in the last chapter indicate that progress has been made in the organization of curricular access for children with learning difficulties in secondary schools. There are no simple solutions and the problems should not be underestimated. As the HMI secondary school survey concluded: 'it is not easy to provide the necessary combination of specialist skills and knowledge either in a single teacher or through the cooperative working of two teachers', and went on the refer to the largely unsolved problem of sustaining a curricular programme for the less able while taking account of their difficulties through the teaching skills employed.

There has, however, been progress in conceiving a common curriculum which might be sufficient to embrace the needs of pupils with mild learning difficulties and some of the children with moderate difficulties. A DES publication in 1977, commonly referred to as the Red Book, discussed a common curriculum for 11- to 16-year olds and offered a checklist of eight areas of experience which ought to be provided within a balanced curriculum: aesthetic/creative; ethical; linguistic; mathematical; physical; scientific; social/political; spiritual. Although at first glance the areas seem to correspond to particular subjects, the checklist is also useful as a means of examining how any subject may in some measure provide opportunities for each type of experience. It would be difficult to deny that the education of slow learners has sometimes not been a balanced one in terms of this checklist, partly because other pressing needs have appeared to have priority.

Two further booklets in 1981 and 1983 discussed progress in conceiving a common curriculum in the course of a co-operative venture which began in 1977 between five LEAs, 41 schools and their staff and a group of HMIs. In essence, it was a study of curriculum development identifying 'what needs to go on in schools if a common curriculum, *appropriately interpreted according to individual need*, is to be introduced for much of the week for *all* pupils to 16' (emphases added). It was subtitled 'Towards a statement of entitlement' – a statement of the curriculum which all children are entitled to.

While the exercise took the eight areas of experience as a starting point and as a continuing theme, the 1983 report is rich in detail about aims ('easy to state but difficult to live up to'), objectives and the implication of the latter for more flexible forms of assessment. The aims identified by schools were essentially elaborations of those referred to earlier. It was in the definition of objectives that it became possible to perceive how low achievers may experience a common curriculum.

It would be fair to suggest that the curriculum has tended to be viewed as the content and information to be taught – as a body of knowledge. Those involved in the inquiry found it useful to identify objectives in terms of skills, concepts, attitudes and knowledge. In doing so they made a bridge between the nature of the curriculum and the needs of the learner. We have customarily defined the learner's difficulties in terms of weaknesses in acquiring skills and concepts, in developing appropriate attitudes as well as knowledge. If curriculum objectives are defined in these terms *and* moreover are assessed in them rather than in the end product of a conventionally examined possession of a body of information and content, we are at least some way towards seeing how the common curriculum can meet the needs of children with learning difficulties.

Skills were distinguished as: communication, numerical, observational, imaginative (e.g. putting oneself in other situations, whether of time, place or person), physical and practical, social (to co-operate, negotiate, consider other points of view, recognize non-verbal communications), problem solving and creative, organizational and study skills. As well as considering the place of these skills in the teaching of particular departments and across departments, assessment can be based on performance on different kinds of task and response.

Attitudes are dispositions to think or act in particular ways in relation to oneself, other individuals and groups, for example, adaptability, co-operation, self-confidence, empathy, curiosity – difficult to define and assess but no less important than skills and concepts.

Concepts are the means for organizing, classifying and understanding experience and knowledge, for interpreting new experience and making connections between one area of study and another.

Concepts are numerous, some of wide application (e.g. continuity; energy), others specific to particular studies. The suggestion was made that a school should identify concepts important generally in its curriculum, that each department should identify concepts specific to its teaching and that departments might identify concepts occurring across departments. This is particularly important in teaching less able children and an important feature of curriculum plans in special schools.

Knowledge is the information selected to develop skills, concepts and attitudes in order to achieve curricular aims. The criteria for selection of content are, of course, many. They include the eight areas of experience as well as the locality and neighbourhood of the school and the community it serves, the needs of pupils and of course the teaching interests and strengths of departments and individual teachers.

The schools which had taken part in this demanding curriculum exercise then found themselves faced with the next question which has no doubt occurred to the reader. How will such a curriculum be assessed? Clearly, the curriculum objectives which have been referred to could not be adequately assessed by means of a traditional formal examination although there would be some place for it in content areas and with pupils of average and above ability. Some form of continuous assessment would be required. Schools in one area analysed their objectives and identified specific tasks related to them which could be assessed by a range of techniques – practical, oral and written tasks as well as observational records by teachers. This proved useful in helping to determine the teaching and learning programme as well as a more informative basis for records and reports. Some of the publications from the Further Education Curriculum Unit include profiles and skill sequences which would be relevant to some of the attitudes, practical and social skills that might be assessed. The involvement of pupils in the assessment process is also desirable – 'if pupils are to value the curriculum to which teachers say they are entitled, they will have to be taken into teacher's confidence and be allowed to discuss what it is that they are entitled to experience. They should also be given the opportunity to comment on how, and how much, they are learning' (DES, 1983).

In summary, the curriculum may be viewed not simply as the subjects of which it is comprised but also as the skills, concepts and attitudes which it aims to develop. The idea of a common curriculum which caters for all children including those with special educational needs does not imply that all should be expected to learn to the same range and depth of content but should have the opportunity for learning which extends over the eight areas of experience and for the realization of the aims of education through the development, so far as they are able, of skills, concepts, attitudes and knowledge.

There are of course many problems in teaching a common curriculum. There is the obvious problem presented by very poor levels of reading, written work and in some subjects of poor numeracy. Teachers are probably less aware of the difficulties presented by the language of instruction – not only the language the teacher uses but the language of textbooks which may hold difficulties even to normal readers. Perera (1981) suggests in fact that difficulties in understanding the language of workcards and textbooks are more prevalent and serious than those which the teacher's spoken language may cause since the latter is accompanied by gestures and facial expression and the teacher is also able to respond to misunderstandings. She gives some nice examples of words such as *caravan* being used in a context and sense quite different from the one you would think of if you had travelled on a motorway in the summer. Apart from the ubiquitous problem of technical terms which afflict even students of education, there is the use of formal vocabulary, e.g. *locate* instead of *find; afford* instead of *provide* or *have; in excess of* instead of *more than* or *higher than.* The problems presented by sentence patterns which are less frequent in speech than in writing are numerous and are familiar to readers of textbooks and newspapers when the construction starts to convey the wrong meaning and it is necessary to read the sentence again. Perera gives many examples drawn from school textbooks.

It is perhaps even more difficult to appreciate the difficulty which children have in understanding. One assumes that children of secondary age have reached a stage of mental development when they should be able to reason and comprehend at the level that the subjects of the curriculum demand. A good deal of research has shown that even children of average ability are still developing the ability to solve problems and to make judgements about content. Peel (1972) and others working with him have presented pupils with passages drawn from texts in history, geography, science, social studies, and have posed questions, the responses to which reveal the maturity of their explanations and judgements. Even well into the teens, some pupils' responses were classified as illogical or tautological, e.g. contradicting other information in the passage or something which the child had already said. At the next level, a simple explanation is restricted to information in the passage or to what is observable in an experiment – perhaps also bringing in some other information. At the next level, which is increasingly required in the secondary curriculum, the pupil is able to consider a range of possibilities, to make a hypothesis or explanation and to test it against the evidence. It is a quality of thinking which partly depends upon a range of concepts and knowledge, partly also on practice and experience of thinking round topics rather than simply assimilating information. It also depends partly on language competence for expressing possibilities and making qualifications and judgements.

The response of slow learners to curriculum content is likely to be at the lower levels of that scale – although they sometimes reveal greater capacity to make judgements about situations in which they have interest and experience. Though their starting point is low, it is not inevitable that it should remain so. This is one of several reasons why there has been a trend in many areas of the curriculum to select content related to pupils' experience and interests. Methods of teaching have become more active, employing discovery and inquiry, providing more opportunity for discussion.

In a survey of the extent to which Schools Council Curriculum Project Materials were suited to the needs of slow learners, Gulliford and Widlake (1975) concluded that many were suitable for the above reasons and that some could have been more accessible if the reading demands had been reduced. Even so there were many examples of interesting work and certain projects such as the Moral Education Project (*Lifelines*) (McPhail, 1972) and Language in Use (Doughty, 1971), which could be mainly oral, were very appropriate.

A survey of the curricular needs of slow learners (Brennan, 1979) involved 500 primary, secondary and special schools nominated by LEAs as doing successful work. Evaluation of their success in particular subjects indicated that in primary schools, English, environmental studies and mathematics were most frequently successful. In secondary and special schools, apart from reading and English, courses which had relevance to post-school life (leavers' courses, parenthood, home economics, social service) were more likely to be rated successful than those in science, history, geography and humanities generally. The latter are, of course, subjects in which the reading of texts and other resources is important as well as writing; they require the understanding of abstract concepts and the ability to reason and make judgements. Yet no specialist teacher, convinced of the value of their subject for enlarging pupils' awareness of the world in which they live, for enriching their lives in some measure and certainly as an educative medium for developing thought and feeling, would be happy to see it neglected. The problem, of course, is how to teach it especially in a situation where the needs of able children must also be provided for.

There are no simple answers but it is encouraging that, over the whole curriculum field, publications have been appearing addressed to this issue. The Schools Council project 'Geography for the Young Leaver' was prepared with the needs of average and less able pupils in mind. The themes 'Man, land and leisure', 'Cities and people', 'People, places and work' and the variety of materials and approaches contributed to wide acceptance and use. Boardman (1982) and Williams (1982) have discussed the teaching of geography to slow learners, the former publication also including accounts by teachers, and both make reference to other publications on the topic.

The field of history teaching has been well served by a Historical Association publication by Cowie (1979) which relates an account of slow learners' difficulties to the objectives and practice of teaching – the use of oral work, books, visual material, TV and radio, written work, simulations and games, field work and museum visits – and also considers what history might be taught. Hallam has undertaken research into the thinking of children and adolescents about historical topics and has also considered the teaching of slow learners (Hallam, 1982). If anyone doubts that history can genuinely be taught to children with moderate learning difficulties, an article by Tate (1979), 'How can we re-create the past?', should dispel the doubts. The most extensive publication to date is a handbook for teachers prepared by Northern Ireland teachers which covers everything from worksheets to computers, from history trails to the use of the Public Record Office, all considered in relation to the teaching of slow learners in secondary schools (McIver, 1982).

The HMI primary survey found that few primary schools had effective programmes for teaching science. Although a fair proportion of classes were introduced to plants, animals and objects intended to stimulate interest and inquiry, there were few in which the work was planned to develop the perception of relationships, cause and effects, notions of stability and change, simple problem solving. A useful feature of the Schools Council project Science 5–13 was the attempt to define objectives for aspects such as observation, questioning, concepts, interests and communication at different levels of thinking development. The objectives and the suggested activities would have relevance to younger low attainers in the secondary school. There is a continuation project called Learning Through Science.

The teaching of science with slow learners in the secondary school has been reviewed by Kershaw (1978) and Hinson and Hughes (1982). Useful reviews of science schemes are included in *Ways and Means 2* (Taylor, 1981), including three designed to meet the needs of less able fourth- and fifth-year pupils: *Science at Work; LAMP;* and *Open Science.*

There has been considerable development in recent years in methods and resources for enhancing personal and social education – important for all pupils but perhaps particularly so for those with special needs. As a Schools Council working party defined it: personal and social education includes the teaching and informal activities which are planned to enhance the development of knowledge, understanding, attitudes and behaviour concerned with (i) oneself and others; (ii) social institutions, structures and organization; and (iii) social and moral issues. It depends of course not only upon opportunities for learning and experience within the curriculum but for informal learning and the experience provided by the ethos of the school. Group tutoring (Button, 1982) and active tutorial work (Lancashire Education Committee, 1980) provide a rationale and structure for practice which many teachers have been enthusiastic about as a basis for form tutorial work in a pastoral setting. Within the curriculum, many subjects and activities contribute to personal and social development. English, drama, creative work and discussion in any subject provide pupils with opportunity to express ideas and feelings, developing their own ideas and awareness of other points of view. The latter is much to the fore in the moral education curriculum materials (McPhail, 1972), the first part being entitled *In Other People's Shoes*. Stimulus cards present situations which aim to develop through adolescents' responses a greater awareness and sensitivity to others' needs, feelings and interests. Others explore the consequences of actions and events in everyday situations. Health education, which encompasses a wide field from basic information to feelings, relationships and moral concerns, has been well provided for by Schools Council projects covering the age ranges 5 to 13 and 13 to 18 (Williams, 1980). Religious education, social studies, leavers' preparation, social and life-skills courses may each contribute, some through the development of personal competencies, others through the development of a sense of self in relation to others.

It should not be overlooked that BBC and Independent Television provide an extensive menu of programmes covering the whole range of the curriculum. Some of the out-put has the needs of less successful or reluctant learners in mind and many of those which do not do so explicitly provide visual material which can be an experience from which pupils will gain something and which will be a stimulus to classroom discussion at a suitable level.

List of further reading

BARNES, D. (1982). *From Communication to Curriculum*. Harmondsworth: Penguin.

BRENNAN, W.K. (1985). *Curriculum for Special Needs*. Milton Keynes: Open University Press.

GRIFFIN, D. (1978). *Slow Learners: a break in the circle*. London: Woburn Press.

JONES DAVIES, C. (Ed) (1975). *The Slow Learner in the Secondary School*. London: Ward Lock.

WIDLAKE, P. (1983). *How to Reach the Hard to Teach*. Milton Keynes: Open University Press.

CHAPTER 6
Basic Educational Skills

Difficulties in learning to read

The number of children who have considerable difficulty in learning to read at the usual time in the early years of the primary school is surprisingly large as figures given in Chap. 1 show. Some learn to read sufficiently well during the primary years but others need continuing individual help; some arrive at secondary school with reading levels below that of average nine-year olds, posing the problems discussed in Chaps. 3 and 4 of how to organize special help as well as enabling them to have the experience of a normal curriculum. The problem is also one for further and adult education in the increasing curricular provision for those with poor academic attainments and in the organization of literacy schemes. The Adult Literacy and Basic Skills Unit (DES, 1983) reported that in 1981, there were over 100,000 students receiving tuition in groups or individually. The number of people who are not functionally literate is estimated by the Unit to be around two million.

The reasons for this state of affairs must be a question in the minds of anyone new to the field; it continues to puzzle those who have spent much of their time teaching poor readers. It is tempting to seek some basic cause or causes and to seek some specific remedy. Perhaps the problem stems from the inconsistencies of English orthography – the way letters and combinations of letters represent words in the English language – deriving as it does from Anglo-Saxon, Latin, Norman French. Bernard Shaw, of course, left money to get English spelling reformed. There was indeed in the 1960s an interesting and well-conducted trial of a modified alphabet, the initial teaching alphabet (i.t.a.), designed by Sir James Pitman. It consists of 44 characters, 24 of them from the traditional orthography or alphabet (t.o.) omitting 'x' and 'q'. The additional characters are combinations of two letters which in t.o. form common digraphs such as *th, sh, ie, ee, ea.* There are three forms of the letter *a* for different sounds as in *cat, angel, farm.* Upper case letters are always just larger editions of the lower case letters. It left 50 per cent of t.o. words unchanged. The aim was that the modified alphabet would be used as an initial medium of instruction and that once children became fluent it would be easy for them to transfer to t.o.

The evidence showed that children made faster progress through their reading scheme in i.t.a., appeared to develop written work of better quality and had little difficulty in the transition to t.o. The evidence was less clear in the case of slow learners (Downing, 1969). That i.t.a. has not been widely adopted is probably due to the problem of providing the wide range of reading material in i.t.a. which infant teachers look for (Bullock Report, paras. 7.27–29; Southgate *et al.*, 1981).

It is interesting in this connection that severe reading difficulties are said to be rare in Japan even though their writing system looks complicated to us and consists of more than 2,000 ideographs (figures representing an idea) derived historically from Chinese as well as 51 basic symbols giving a regular representation of phonetic syllables, each one representing a consonant plus vowel. Sakamoto (1978) in a readily accessible chapter describes how children starting school have often already acquired many of these phonetic symbols and that parents take great interest in their progress. The ideographs are learnt gradually during the school years.

A modified alphabet would reduce one source of difficulty but there are plenty of others. In viewing the problems of learning to read, an analogy may be helpful. Many adults express with regret that although they had piano lessons as a child, they did not get very far and eventually gave it up. Failure to learn the piano has not been subjected to the intensive study that failure in reading has but it is not difficult to identify some of the factors involved. First of all, it is a skill which doesn't come easily; it requires persistence, practice and a perception of the goal; a background of interest in music in the home – as well of encouragement and support – is obviously extremely important. Even so, most children find other activities with bikes, bats and balls more rewarding and less effortful. The piano teacher is obviously crucial. They need to be kind, concerned, encouraging, interested in the learner as a person yet suitably demanding, systematic, and clear about how the skill is learnt and may be best taught. Of course, the child may not be cut out for learning the piano. There are no doubt specific difficulties in interpreting the notation, visually and cognitively, from the page and in translating these into the finger movements and combining the whole complex mental and physical operation. Sometimes, matters are made worse by exercises and scales which don't seem to have much to do with playing an enjoyable tune. It is obviously a difficult, long-term task and if you don't like it, you can give it up.

If you don't learn to read at the usual time you have to keep at it in spite of frustration and limited rewards; you search for the hidden key to reading and probably lose the flexibility of the younger learner to the variety of sources of information in the text which consititutes reading. A succession of teachers seek to maintain your motivation, create some success and attempt to identify the skills you lack. Should there be more exercises and drills? Or should we settle for 'playing some simple enjoyable tunes' in the hope that the skills will be put together?

There are no simple explanations for failure in learning to read. It is a complex set of skills dependent upon many mental abilities and processes – language, perception, memory, thinking – and requires sufficient motivation and other personal characteristics in the pupil. Equally important is well-organized teaching, based on a sound knowledge of the process of learning to read, through which different kinds of skill are developed at different stages. Failure may best be viewed as a result of multiple interacting factors in the child and the teaching process. When children learn early and well, the process seems almost as natural as learning to talk and walk; at the other extreme, it is a perpetual source of frustration which tends to exacerbate the problem by confirming inappropriate responses and the negative feelings created by failure. The problem for the helping teacher – and also an opportunity – is to find a way of releasing the pupil from their impasse.

The process of learning to read

A popular conception of how children learn to read is that they are taught to recognize words at sight and that they can be helped to read new or unfamiliar words by learning phonics, i.e. the system by which the sounds of spoken words are represented in letters and combinations of letters in printed or written words. The 'methods' of teaching reading have sometimes been reduced to a sterile argument about the merits of 'look and say' or whole word methods and phonics. In fact, the majority of teachers teach both visual recall of words and an appreciation of the relationships between sounds and symbols, usually in the context of sentences drawn from children's experiences and early reading books. But as Marie Clay (1972) stated categorically: 'As explanations of what we do when we read, the terms "look and say", sight words and phonics are nonsense. Reading is more complex than that.' She points out that all readers from the competent five-year-old to the efficient adult use the sense of what they are reading; the sentence structure; the order of words, letters and ideas; the size of words and letters; special features of sound, shape or layout; special knowledge from past experience. Children learning to read develop *strategies* for interpreting print using a variety of sources of information in the printed sentence. The problem for the teacher of reading is how to teach so that the child is helped to develop flexible strategies rather than trying to read by relying on visual memory for the word or on phonic analysis of its letters. The problem for the backward reader is that they have not developed efficient strategies possibly because the teaching did not match their need at some point in the process of learning, possibly because of some delay or weakness in the mental processes involved, possibly because they were not emotionally ready to attend and persist in a difficult task.

Most children come to school with a sufficient vocabulary and a basic competence in the linguistic patterns of English. They begin the process of learning to read by realizing how language and ideas may be represented in written or printed symbols, the flow of spoken language being separated into printed words. Teachers use a variety of methods – such as sentence captions written beneath children's pictures or sentences suggested by children being composed from a vocabulary of frequent words on cards – to make children aware of words, their order and the message of a sentence. They begin to pay attention to some of the features of the code – long and short words, letters and combinations of letters – within the representation of the sentence. Later they need to learn more about the system by which the sounds of words are represented by letters and combinations of letters. It is a complicated code especially in English where the relationships between sound and symbols are not so regular as in some languages. If reading were only a matter of learning to decode these sound-symbol relationships, reading would be an extremely difficult task indeed.

Fortunately, children do not learn to read simply by mastering the code. They use the visual information from print and whatever phonic awareness they have in relation to the language of the message expressed in the text since these provide clues both of meaning and the linguistic structure of the sentence. The meaning of the sentence may be suggested by the context of the activity in which reading takes place or by what has just been read in previous sentences. As the reader gets into the sentence, its meaning begins to unfold giving a powerful indication of the remaining words. Similarly, the linguistic structure of the sentence supports and guides the reading. For example, in the sentence 'The boys are playing in the park', after *boys* the reader would anticipate *are* rather than *is* and after *are* would anticipate *playing* rather then *played*. There is a range of possibilities for the final word – garden, house, park, playground, etc. If the reader selected *playground*, we would correct them but would notice the probability that they had used their awareness of the letter *p*. In short, the reader is anticipating what words are coming in the sentence, using their awareness of meaning and the patterns of language. They check what they anticipate by looking for clues in the print – short and long words, initial letters, final letters and any other features which give them information.

Learning to read

On entry to school, children vary in their language competence, their experience of books, stories, play and educational materials and in their readiness for settling to school tasks and activities.

Some may have started to read already; others require a period – sometimes a prolonged one – of settling in, of developing visual discrimination with pictures and patterns, of listening to stories being read and, through nursery rhymes and jingles, awareness of the sounds of words. Even for children with good language development, thinking of the flow of language as something which can be separated as words and realizing how words can be represented as marks in sequence on a page is not easy. They may be uncertain what reading and writing are. Reid (1966) in an influential and interesting paper drew attention to children's confused notions. From talking to children at this stage, she was led to comment that compared with learning to ride a bicycle, reading is initially a mysterious activity for many children. Perhaps it continues so for some.

The most common approach in beginning reading is a 'language-experience' method. An activity which children have enjoyed will be talked about and represented in children's paintings. The teacher puts a sentence caption beneath it and reads it; children 'read' it back. In due course, children make their own personal books. A picture of something in their experience is talked about and the teacher writes a sentence beneath the child's picture, reading it to them and suggesting that they trace over the words, later copying it. As other pictures are made, the book becomes their first 'reading book' through which words begin to be recognized. The child's sentences may be written on card and cut up into phrases or words to be recombined or used for word matching. Some of the words will be those in the beginning book of the reading scheme and the teacher will introduce others to prepare children for it.

A variation of this language-experience approach was developed in a Schools Council project called 'Breakthrough to Literacy' (Mackay *et al.*, 1970). Since it has been quite widely used in remedial teaching as well as with infants, it is worth comparing with what has just been outlined. Like infant teachers, the project team believed that the reading material should be based on the child's own language and experience.

The child begins therefore by composing and reading their own sentences which express something in their recent experience. They do this using a Sentence Maker which consists of a folder with pockets in which are alphabetically stored a collection of cards with words, word endings and punctuation marks printed on them, making up a collection of 130 items. The printed words are those which have been found to be commonly used by young children in this activity but there are also blank cards on which the teacher can print other words which the child's 'message' requires. A plastic stand is provided into which the word-cards can be slotted to make up the sentence. There is also a large version of the materials which teachers can use with classes or groups. A magnet board with figurines assists with language activities, nursery rhymes and stories.

In composing their own sentence on the sentence maker, the child has to select the words from the folder and in placing them in the slotted holder perceives through their actions that the words are sequenced from left to right in the order of speaking them and becomes aware of differences in size and appearance. When they replace the cards in the folder, they do so by matching them with the printed words in the allotted places. They also write their sentence in their book and illustrate it with a picture.

Clay (1979), who has written some very perceptive books on how children learn to read and how teachers can assist the process, argues strongly that children should try to write their own sentences rather than just copy them since the process of attempting to change spoken words into written symbols is an invaluable learning experience. One is reminded of children's first messages to Father Christmas, the spelling of which cannot but cause a parental smile, combined with pleasure and admiration that they had succeeded in conveying their urgent request. In fact, infant children normally do a lot of creative writing and the teacher selects common words which are incorrectly coded and prints the correct form above. Clay specifically warns against the view that the less competent child should be saved from creative writing by being allowed to trace, copy or fill in spaces on duplicated sheets. Her point might be considered in relation to the idiosyncratic spelling in written work by junior and secondary slow learners. It may appear to be poor work but what they are trying to express may not be so poor. It is good that they should be encouraged to try to write their ideas since their successes and failures in coding the message tell us something about the help they need. Filling in spaces and worksheets avoids 'illiterate' writing but limits the opportunity to express ideas and to learn the code for doing so.

The Breakthrough materials also provide for phonic work. A Word Maker folder contains small cards each with a symbol (i.e. a letter or a digraph such as *th* or *ch*) representing a sound. In placing symbols in the slotted holder to make up words and in copying and writing them the child is launched on phonics and spelling. The project also prepared 24 first-reading books related to the interests and activities of children and to their linguistic resources by being partly derived from conversation and stories recorded from children.

The most common practice in infant schools is to base the further reading programme on a published reading scheme which has, in addition to the main books, supplementary books and other materials at each level for consolidating learning through careful control of vocabulary, sentence patterns and phonic work. The content of reading schemes has sometimes been criticized for not matching the experience of children and therefore being a factor in the difficulties which some children have. As Mackay *et al*. (1970) expressed it: 'an unimaginatively solid middle class ethos; the adventures of a happy Mummy and a handsome Daddy dealing confidently, if dully, with smiling children, dog- and cat-attended, in a perpetually sunlit garden.' It is possible, of course, to go to the other extreme and provide content which gives children no windows on to a wider experience than their own drab environment. For older backward readers, there is an extensive provision of books with content which the authors perceive as matching teenage social and personal preoccupations. In infant books, there has also been an attempt to avoid the unnatural, artificial language which used to result from the attempt to give a high rate of repetition of 'sight words' or to control the introduction of words exemplifying particular sound-symbol relationships. It is worth examining some reading schemes (and some remedial books) to judge their suitability for qualifying as literature!

With older children, later in primary school or in secondary school, whose reading skill is still at a very limited stage, there is a similar need for reading books with well-controlled vocabulary so that learning is consolidated but progressive. The content needs to be suitable for their age: the books should not look like an infant series.

Individual tutoring with very retarded readers often starts like the infant school approach of making a book on some topic of interest – football, pop groups, oneself – in which the writing of the pupil's own sentences is the means for developing an initial vocabulary of words and the use of context clues before continuing with a reading book suitable in content and interest level. The resource room of a remedial service or the remedial room in a secondary school are places to study the considerable range of books available. Atkinson and Gains (1985) have compiled an A to Z list according to reading levels.

The development of phonic understanding

Great-grandmother probably learnt that see-ay-tee spells cat; grandmother might have learnt that ku-a-tu reads as cat. The modern child is more likely to have been led to see that the same letter at the beginning of cat, can, cap can be heard as the same sound when the words are spoken and similarly to recognize the short vowel sounds *a, e, o, u* in three-letter words that they know and meet often in their reading. As reading proceeds, other letters and digraphs (*th, ch, sh, ea, ee, ay, ow*) are taught with several examples and their use encountered in reading. There is a great range of phonic study books, games, audio-tapes and other resources which assist children to see similarities in the spelling patterns of words and the similarities as they are spoken or heard. Children may go through such activities with only modest gains for their reading; in early reading and remedial reading, children need to be shown how they can use this phonic awareness along with other clues in reading sentences. The bright children generally grasp the principle quickly and start making their own phonic discoveries. The slow learner is less likely to do so. Some older backward readers get stuck by trying to 'unlock' the word letter by letter rather than using the sense of what they are reading and are also likely to get stuck sounding our irregular words.

There is much to be said for teaching or reteaching phonics as opportunity arises in a reading lesson. When there is individual tutoring, words presenting difficulty can be studied to ensure perception of the symbols, hearing and speaking the sound, writing the word and thinking of other examples of the phonic element. The Fernald Kinaesthetic method is generally found to be effective (Fernald, 1943). It employs several sensory channels: visual, auditory, kinaesthetic (V.A.K. method). In plain language, the child *looks* carefully at the word and its constituent syllables and letters while also *saying* the word slowly to promote awareness of the sounds, and *traces* over the letters with a pencil or finger. Younger children like being told to sky-write it, i.e. 'try writing it in the air.' With severely handicapped learners, tactile experience tracing over letters made out of rough material is a further sensory input (VAKT). The word is then covered and written from memory. If incorrect, the process is repeated. The word is then written into the child's vocabulary book. Several accounts of this type of approach with intelligent but reading retarded children may be found in practical chapters by Cotterell (1970).

Teaching phonics well is not a simple task. The first problem is that children vary in their ability to discriminate the sounds of a spoken word whether spoken by the teacher or themselves. (The adult may appreciate this by trying to identify the difference between *th* in *thin* and *this* and the *s* in *sure* and *usual*.) Unless care is taken, a consonant may be voiced and for this reason it has been suggested that consonant sounds might be identified and taught by hearing their sound at the end of words. Then there are all the familiar problems of letters which have different sound values in different spelling patterns (e.g. *man, ball, cake*) and a particular speech sound is often represented in different ways. The long *a* sound is most commonly symbolized in the three forms: *cake, train, play* but there are also *break, vein, eight, straight, they, gauge*. The *or* sound in *horn* is frequently spelt as in *storm, tortoise* but also by *aw* in *saw, draw,* and by *al* in always, *call, salt*. There are also *broad, bought* and *caught*. Everyone knows that there are several spelling patterns for many sounds. In teaching phonics, it is important to be always aware of them. Perusal of phonic workbooks is one way of doing this. Cordts (1965) provides a thorough account of phonics for the teacher of reading.

In spite of the problems, it is widely accepted that the development of phonic knowledge or awareness is a valuable aid to the reading process. The important question is how phonics works in that process. In the first place, phonics teaching in which common patterns are grouped together as word families (*might, fight, light*) promotes *visual* recognition of such words. Knowledge of the common sounds of consonants, vowels and digraphs give clues, which assisted by the context, help the word to be read. The more clues in the word and in the context which the reader is able to try using, the better the chance of getting the word. In the context, there are the clues of meaning and the syntactic structure of the sentence. Intonation is also worth considering. Many older backward readers read in a word-by-word manner in a dull monotone – they are reading isolated words rather than sentences. Reading while listening to a tape or to a good reader helps this. In individual teaching, it is important, of course, to tell the reader a word which is phonically beyond them.

In the secondary curriculum, many terms in subject areas are regular in terms of phonic rules – population, continental, element, atom. The child who has learnt *ch* in words such as *cheese, chop, chin* needs to extend their awareness to *ch* in *chemist, stomach-ache, mechanical, chronicle, chlorophyll*. There are also prefixes and suffixes worth teaching. A useful discussion of phonics at the secondary level is provided by Ann Dubs in Marland (1977).

The development of fluency

Children whose visual recognition of words and use of phonic knowledge develop well soon practise their developing skill in reading a range of books at school and often at home. They become quicker. They begin to read silently. Backward readers usually read slowly, word by word, and usually aloud. Their difficulties don't encourage them to read independently so they don't get the practice which would improve their recognition skills nor, as these improve, their fluency.

When it is judged that a backward reader is ready for becoming more fluent (and this is perhaps a judgement based on the teacher's experience), a number of steps can be taken. First, they should be given reading material which is at a much easier level so that most words are familiar and pauses less likely. It should be interesting, and something which the child understands. It can be a passage which they read several times so that they become thoroughly familiar with it. One ten-year-old was good at making up stories though not good at writing them. His story was recorded, transcribed and typewritten. He was so proud of his typewritten story that he read it to other teachers and took it home to read to his parents. In doing so, he got the 'feel' of real reading – looking ahead to see what was coming in the text, checking a word by the sense of what he was reading. And of course his reading speeded up. The same thing can be done with a passage from a story book and the re-readings timed; the improvements in time are rewarding so long as the emphasis on speed does not result in halts and inaccuracies. Another device in an individual situation is for the tutor to read one page and the pupil the next. Backward readers enjoy this reduction of their labour and some have been known to choose odd or even pages having first ascertained which pages have most pictures and therefore less text! The important thing is that they 'get into' the story, grasp what it is all about and are eager to find what happens next.

Some backward readers at this stage need encouragement to read silently or at least with little vocalization. Some older backward readers have been reading aloud *to* people for so long that reading to themselves is always oral reading. Reading aloud is slower than silent reading; the vocal performance holds the reader back. Some remedial teachers put the text on to audio-tape, and the reader follows it through earphones. There was a man called McDade in Chicago in the 1930s who had beginning reading taught by a non-oral method. It is worth considering how he did it. It might prove useful with a child who has a speech and language disorder (Buswell, 1945).

Paired reading

Children who learn to read more or less at the usual time in the early years of the primary school find their developing skill rewarding and improve it by further reading. Those in whom the skills don't develop or don't integrate so well and those who have little stimulus and encouragement to read, do not get the practice which provides the basis for further reading development.

This is where parents can play a useful part in helping their child through 'paired or shared reading' in which for a short regular time each day a parent and child read together. In general, teachers have been reluctant to involve parents in helping their child since their anxiety for the child 'to get on' may increase negative feelings about the difficulty; in their lack of understanding of how reading is taught, they may emphasize aspects which don't match with what the school is doing. There is some justification for these views when well-intentioned but understandably worried parents try to teach at home. The answer surely is not to discourage it but to explain to parents what they can do and how to do it. In the case of many other parents, we should be concerned about their *apparent* lack of interest and practical help. In fact, in the majority of families, there is concern, especially in the earlier years of schooling.

The essence of paired reading is not teaching but reading to and with the poor reader so that they have a prop which enables them to 'read' and so develop those skills of using the sense of what is being read. Tizard *et al.* (1982) evaluated the effect of parental help in reading over a two-year period. Two classes in different schools had this help during their first two years in junior school and their reading attainment was compared with a control group in the same school. They had achieved a significantly higher level as judged by test results. A similar evaluation was made for the effect of extra teacher help in tutorial groups but their reading was not significantly higher than control classes. The researchers also concluded from their work that such collaboration is feasible in inner-city, multi-racial schools, even if some of the parents are non-literate or non-English speaking. (Also reported by Hewison, 1982.)

Young and Tyre (1983) describe a paired reading scheme in which parents heard their child read a few pages each day for not more than 15 minutes. The instructions were to read the passage to the child, talk about the pictures, people and events, read it again while running a finger under the line of print and to read it again with the child joining in, pausing occasionally for the child to supply the next word. Advice was given about a variety of word games and other activities for another 15 minutes. Initially, the books used were about two years below the levels of reading ability. Parents read to and with their children and heard them read for not more than 15 minutes a day and a further time was allowed for using the passage read as a basis for a variety of word games and other activities. The procedure was for the parent, having read the passage, to talk about the pictures, people and events in the story; then to read it aloud with good expression while running a finger along the line of print. The passage was read again with the child joining in and, on a further reading, pauses were made for the child to supply a word or phrase alone. Finally the child read alone with words being supplied if they hesitated.

Glynn (1980) reporting on paired reading experiments in Birmingham and New Zealand worked with more precise methods of rewarding learning behaviour. Parents were shown how to praise (i) for reading a sentence correctly, (ii) for children correcting themselves after a mistake, (iii) for getting a word correct after prompting. When a child offered a word which did not make sense, there were two alternatives: prompt with clues about the meaning of the story, e.g. ask a question about it, or ask the child to look carefully at the word and to see what part is being wrongly read. If there is no success after the prompts, the child is told the word. The final case is when the child makes no attempt at the word: they are either asked to read on to the end of the sentence or to go back to the beginning again. One of these may result in getting the word from the use of context. Glynn found that in observations of parents' behaviour initially, they tended not to delay their response to errors, usually supplied the word rather than give a prompt and they praised rarely. As a result of training sessions and follow up visits by the teacher, they were able to develop more effective strategies.

There are a number of reports of other schemes of paired reading. Bush (1983) used library books rather than readers in order to encourage children's knowledge of fiction. The initial preparation of parents was partly done by role play demonstrating the contrast between the 'old' methods of helping children which often resulted in tension and the modern approach emphasizing a relaxed and positive approach. Teachers visited homes about five times in an eight-week period. The guidelines allowed children the choice of book and the freedom to discard it if wished; the child chose the time and duration of paired reading. Parents were expected to avoid negative comments and to praise frequently.

Topping and McKnight (1984) have described paired reading in Kirklees where many schools are involved including special schools for children with moderate learning difficulties and also for maladjusted children.

All the accounts report gains in reading attainment and an enthusiastic response from parents and children. It breaks the circle of failure by giving support and help in *reading* rather than engaging in word drills and exercises; it emphasizes success and praise. Equally important is the demonstration of the effectiveness of well-prepared partnership – between parents and children and between home and school. It is not a completely new idea. Schonell experimented with parent-co-operation groups in 1949 and there have always been a few teachers who paired a good reader with a poor one in the same class; or secondary schools where older pupils gave help to younger ones. What is different is that procedures are evolving and paired reading is only one aspect of the increased emphasis on the involvement of parents.

Extending reading skills

It has always been recognized that once children have 'learnt to read' attention needs to be given to the development of comprehension skills and to the promotion of children's pleasure and interest in reading so that they practise and make use of their skill. In recent years, much more attention has been given to this stage and how reading can be extended for different purposes. The Bullock Report identified three main objectives: the ability to cope with the reading required in each area of the curriculum; the reading competence needed as adults in society; reading as a source of pleasure and personal development which will continue throughout life. These three objectives mean that we should see reading development as continuing throughout the school years and, although English and remedial specialists have special knowledge to offer, it is a responsibility of all teachers.

For children with learning difficulties, achievement of the third objective is a basic one since their difficulty in learning to read and their continuing problems do not dispose them to see reading as enjoyable and rewarding. Primary schools usually have a wide range of story and information books of different levels of difficulty which can be arranged or colour coded to assist readers to select appropriate books. Johnson (1973) suggests the five finger test in which the child places a finger on each word they do not know on a page of a book. If they run out of fingers, it is probable that the book is too difficult for easy reading. Visits to children's libraries, visits by children's librarians to schools and involving the interest of parents through book displays and sales are additional ways of stimulating interests in books.

Story reading by the teacher has an important place and especially important for children whose reading has not been good enough for independent reading or who have not been read to at home. One needs continually to remind oneself how much poor readers miss by not being able to read – the vocabulary and language, the knowledge, and the imaginative and emotional experience of identifying with people in the story. Older slow learners often respond to folk tales which one might have thought too young for them. Edward Blishen described in *Roaring Boys: a schoolmaster's agony* (1955) how, as a young teacher with a difficult class, he found that one way to achieve quiet and order was to read a good story. He records trying to conceal the activity when the Head was around lest it would not be considered 'work'. Contemporary heads would take a positive view of reading which aimed to tempt children into reading or which by reading fictional or biographical material brought reality and life to a curriculum topic, e.g. a scientific discovery or historical incident. Several researchers have shown that personal reading declines during the secondary years (Whitehead *et al.*, 1974). Other observations show that reading in school is often reading 'in short bursts' to extract some pieces of information and that there is too little opportunity for personal reading.

The second objective – the reading required in adult life – covers a wide range from official forms, instructions and recipes, to the interpretation and evaluation of sources of information, persuasion and advice. Williams (1976) has written a useful account of reading for the consumer which is relevant to leavers' courses and life-skill programmes.

The reading required in each area of the curriculum (the first objective) has been the subject of discussion and inquiry in recent years. Walker (1974) has written a stimulating and practical short book on the topic and the three Schools Council projects have illuminated the problem and explored ways in which reading skills can be developed and extended.

A widely used resource are reading laboratories, workshops or centres (i.e. boxes or kits) providing activities in literacy and reading comprehension through progressive levels of work with card materials and exercises. They are carefully designed to develop vocabulary, understanding of more complex sentences, use of context clues and various aspects of comprehension such as order, detail, general understanding and inferences. Provision is made for different kinds of reading, e.g. scanning, use of indexes and dictionaries. There are kits available for different ages and reading levels. The Bullock Report expressed some doubts about the value of such kits since they believed that reading is most rewarding and effective when the individual has a personal reason for reading, is reading within a context and carries his or her own attitudes and values into the reading and is not simply responding passively to the text. Completing tasks in a narrow context does not mean that the ability will transfer to other reading. The Nottingham Schools Council project on extending reading demonstrated, however, that a reading laboratory can have a beneficial effect on the development of effective reading (Lunzer and Gardner, 1979). A structured programme 'enables the student to deploy his newly developed abilities in the context of an open-ended style of teaching.' The researchers stress of course that the use of a kit is only a partial answer – they suggest that an appropriate level of kit might be used for a term in the first year and again for a term in the third year.

The Schools Council project directed by Lunzer and Gardner into the effective use of reading at the secondary stage involved observations of the use of reading in classrooms in a large number of schools – topic work, worksheets, homework – and also explored the use of discussion activities and reading kits. Their major conclusion was that it is not particularly useful to view reading comprehension as composed of separate skills such as the understanding of words in context, making inferences and drawing conclusions. They see it as essentially the ability and willingness to reflect, i.e. making sense of what has been read; comparing this with what one already knows; making judgements about it; finally, revising one's ideas. This conception is very different from the type of comprehension exercise which requires the identification and reproduction of ideas and information from the text. It might be thought too demanding for poor readers and less intelligent children but the methods they have explored make use of discussion in groups or pairs which would be feasible in relation to reading matter of a suitable level of difficulty. As Peel (1972) and others have shown, many children explain incidents from everyday situations as well as from subject areas in a manner restricted to the information given. They do not consider other possibilities or draw upon other experience. An oral discussion approach to thinking about text would be very appropriate to their needs (see p. 95).

In a further study, Lunzer and Gardner (1982) develop this reflective concept by examining a variety of ways of promoting 'directed activity to texts' (with the acronym, DARTS). These fall into two types: *analysing* the text (for example, by underlining, segmenting, labelling, ranking paragraphs in order, listing, tabulating and other ways of examining it); *reconstructing* the text (for example, the use of Cloze technique in which deleted words are replaced through class or group discussion, putting passages into an appropriate sequence); and *prediction* (for example, given part of a story or description of an event, attempting to anticipate or predict what is going to happen).

The readability of texts

One other aspect of the Lunzer and Gardner project was an inquiry into the readability of school texts. They concluded that in addition to the conceptual demands of textbooks and worksheets, learning is often made more difficult by the language in which they are written. They mention that materials in science and social studies make particular demands on pupils especially in the lower years of the secondary school and that special attention to this is needed with pupils whose motivation is low.

Teachers will have no difficulty in appreciating the point being made. We all have experience of being expected to read official documents, reports, or textbooks which are not inviting to read and which are difficult to comprehend at first reading. We may well give up, unless the meaning is important to us personally in some way. It is less easy for a teacher to assess whether material which looks easy to them is suitable or too difficult to, say, 12-year-olds, particularly as the range of ability and reading attainment is quite wide. Experience of teaching brings, of course, awareness of concepts which classes of different ages find difficult and also of the appearance of materials. Adults are often not so aware in oral and written communication of the difficulty which may be caused by the vocabulary and language structures used. One of the benefits of using readability measures is that one becomes rather more aware of this.

There are a number of readability measures which can be used to assess the difficulty of texts alongside teachers' own judgements. Most of them take hundred-word samples of text at random and for each obtain the average sentence length as a measure of sentence complexity. There are two ways of estimating the difficulty of vocabulary. Several formulae establish the number of syllables per hundred words since a textbook with many difficult or technical terms is likely to have longer words. The earliest formula using a syllable count was by Rudolf Flesch and several others have followed: the FOG Index, SMOG (Simple Measure of Gobbledygook) and the Fry Graph from which the grade or age level can be read off the chart. A British procedure which teachers have found easy to use is the Mugford Readability chart which charts words according to word length and the number of syllables (the procedure is given in Lunzer and Gardner (1979) and in Taverner (1980)).

Another way of estimating the 'difficulty' of vocabulary is to count the number of words not on a word list. Thus the Spache Formula for assessing primary reading books has a list of 769 words which was compiled from words which had been shown to be the most frequent in written material as well as also most frequent in the spoken vocabulary of children. The Dale–Chall formula which is useful at the secondary level has a 3,000 word list also obtained from frequency counts. Although this appears laborious, the process of checking 'unfamiliar' words speeds up with practice since it becomes necessary to check only words where one is uncertain. There are also computer packages available which enable the results from several formulae to be obtained for the same passages.

The methods which have been referred to are estimating readability from measures of the text and must be considered 'rough and ready' in view of the many variable factors which affect the reading and comprehension of particular groups of pupils. The Cloze procedure, however, more directly assesses pupils' ability to read and comprehend by requiring them to replace words which have been deleted from a passage, usually every seventh or tenth word. While teachers would wish to accept reasonable alternatives, for the purposes of this assessment only the deleted word is accepted. About 40 per cent correct insertions is taken to indicate a satisfactory level of readability for the group tested. It is a procedure which is useful in writing material for school use and for checking the effect of modifications and rewriting.

Assessment of reading

The teaching of reading with all pupils, and especially with those who are having difficulties, requires a continuing informal assessment and record of progress. As children are heard reading, a record of common words and important sound–symbol associations which appear not to be known provides a basis for individualized help. Equally important are assessment of progress in using contextual clues in reading, the extent to which the reader is understanding what they are reading, whether the reading is slow or fast and whether accurate or uncertain. The reader's motivation for reading and attitude to the task are obviously of great significance.

The knowledgeable and experienced teacher of reading is, one might say, programmed to search for such information in order to plan further stages in reading. Formal procedures of various kinds can assist less experienced teachers to make an assessment of progress and to provide reading material of a suitable level.

The *informal reading inventory* assesses the suitability of reading material by assessing whether the reader is at one of three levels: independent, instructional, frustration. The reader may be considered to be at the *independent* level if, when reading aloud, there is no more than one error in 100 words and there is 90 per cent comprehension. A book to be read for enjoyment and practice should ideally be at this level. The *instructional* level would be indicated by no more than five errors in 100 words and 75 per cent comprehension, e.g. three out of four questions on the text satisfactorily answered. Reading at this level might be expected with instruction to reach the independent level. The *frustration* level is indicated by ten or more errors in 100 words and comprehension below 50 per cent.

Many poor readers have too much experience at the frustration level. In trying to improve their reading, we should find material which is at the instructional level. To give them some sense of 'real reading' and its satisfactions, we should try also to ensure that they have books at the independent level. It might also be helpful to think of a semi-independent level when parents (or peers or teacher or a tape) read with them so that they get the satisfactions of reading even if they are not quite independent.

Another procedure is termed a miscue analysis. The child reads a passage of about 200 to 300 words and a record is made of the following errors: refusals (no response); substitutions; omissions; hesitations (pauses before reading the word); repetition (reading the word twice); insertions (adding a word or part of a word); reversal (e.g. of the order of words); self-correction. A further analysis is made of the substitutions classifying them as:

grapho-phonemic if the miscue resembles the word in at least one phoneme (sound);

syntactic if the miscue fits grammatically;

semantic if the miscue makes good sense in the sentence.

Even if the word is incorrect, it is more promising if the miscue shows use of all three sources of information. If the reader concentrates on the phonic structure of the word and ignores both the meaning and the grammatical structure of the sentence, it would clearly be desirable to encourage them to 'guess' what the word might be – for example, to read the beginning of the sentence again and try reading on to the end in order to get help from the sentence pattern and its meaning.

Sometimes an intelligent pupil with reading difficulties makes frequent mistakes but ploughs through the sentence and, having grasped the meaning, goes back to self-correct misread words. We would encourage them to continue with this strategy of using to the maximum their intelligent guesswork since it will help them 'to get by'. At the same time, we would aim to develop their awareness and recognition of frequent phonic patterns and parts of words so that they could make greater use of grapho-phonemic cues. Encouragement, sympathetic support and increasing success might be expected to effect a considerable improvement though they might well regress in a stressful situation.

Too many poor readers, alas, are so convinced that reading means deciphering the parts of a word that the meaning of what they have read and what might be anticipated ahead goes completely out of mind.

Standardized tests

Compared with this qualitative assessment of a pupil's reading, objective tests may be less informative as a basis for planning remedial help, although some information can be gleaned from them and some group reading tests are designed to assess progress in more advanced reading skills.

The Bullock Report found that Word Recognition tests (Schonell, Burt, Vernon) were the most frequently used. They require the reading of isolated words and the number read yields a word recognition or reading age. They give an indication of the child's progress in immediate recognition of words and also how attempts are made to decipher unknown words. Since there is no context, it is an unsatisfactory method. For example, if progress in learning to read were to be assessed by a word recognition test at the beginning and end of a year, it might be that only six more words were read, i.e. six months' gain in a year. It could be, however, that remedial teaching had encouraged the reader to use the meaning and grammatical cues in reading. Any progress in that aspect of reading skill might not be measured by a recognition test.

For this reason, some teachers have always selected sentence reading tests in preference to word recognition tests but these have the disadvantage of having as many different contexts as there are sentences. Sentence tests commonly require the selection of the appropriate word from five alternatives to complete the sentence.

Assuming that the reader has reached a seven-year level, an individual test of reading comprehension such as the Neale Analysis of Reading is to be preferred – though it has to be said that it is a test reaching the end of its useful life (Vincent *et al.*, 1983). It has three equivalent forms each with six stories. Errors may be recorded according to their type. Comprehension is assessed by questions requiring recall of information. Three scores are obtained: Accuracy (number of errors); Comprehension and Speed of Reading. Comparison of the three scores sometimes has significance for remedial work. For example, a very slow but accurate reader requires attempts to increase the speed of reading (such as that described on p. 109).

Well-constructed reading tests of defined reading abilities are available for reading levels beyond the early stages of learning to read. A review of reading tests (Vincent *et al.*, 1983) is a useful and sound source of information.

There are many sets of 'diagnostic' materials, particularly those which require the reading of words grouped according to the degree and type of phonic complexity. The reader's performance indicates gaps in phonic 'knowledge' as a basis for phonic work. An alternative, of course, is to base phonic study on difficulties noted in the course of reading to the teacher.

Spelling difficulties

Attitudes towards faulty spelling have become more relaxed than formerly, reflecting the belief that children should be encouraged to enjoy expressing themselves without being inhibited by fear of the consequences of spelling mistakes. We have also moved away from spelling as an exercise in isolation to spelling as an activity closely related to the words children need for their written work within the curriculum. This does not mean that spelling does not need to be taught or that children can be left to pick up spelling from their reading. Every school should have a policy for spelling so that pupils are helped to realize that correct spelling of frequently used words is important and that there is a procedure for learning new words and words that they have spelt incorrectly.

There is a particular need for attention to spelling with pupils who are retarded in reading. In giving additional help for reading, it is easy to concentrate on the reading with insufficient attention to spelling and spontaneous writing. Phonic work in reading and study in spelling of words with similar patterns complement and reinforce each other; attention to handwriting is a further aid.

There are, however, those cases where there is a severe spelling disability sometimes associated with specific reading difficulties and sometimes in children whose reading is quite good. Some children seem to have a marked difficulty in keeping the sequence of letters, or have poor visual memory or difficulty in associating speech sounds with their spelling patterns. A study of their spelling errors may suggest a particular emphasis in teaching them. For example, an intelligent first-year secondary pupil made the following errors:

gueniune	colered (coloured)
signiture	probelem

exersizes	scicors	(scissors)
prolog	scarcley	
cortius (courteous)	receite	(receipt)

He makes intelligent attempts to listen to the sound in words and to transcribe them phonically. He gets some, but not enough help from visual memory of the word. As a first step, training in looking at the word to be learnt, visualizing it, perhaps tracing over it, then writing it from memory could be tried.

In helping poor spellers, one becomes aware of a number of aspects which may have significance in particular cases. For example, spelling errors may reflect faulty pronunciation or speech immaturities or defects. In remedial work, attention to speech and language improvement is indicated and specifically to saying words slowly and clearly in syllables as they are being learnt.

Some children, especially younger ones, may be poor in auditory discrimination (e.g. 'ball' for 'bell', 'rak' for 'rag', 'nuber' for 'number'). Recognizing and finding words that rhyme or which contain the same sound should help auditory awareness and support the teaching of words with particular spelling patterns.

Some children transpose letters reversing the sequence or reverse letters such as *b, d.* In others, poor spelling seems likely to be related to poor handwriting – inefficient letter formation, bad spacing of words, confusions about capital and small letters, clumsy writing movements. Such children get poor visual impressions of the words they have written and lack the helpful kinaesthetic impressions obtained from the movements of writing the word.

While a scrutiny of spelling errors can be useful in individual cases, the priority issue is how spelling should be taught. If a group of adults are asked to recall how they were taught spelling in school, two responses are common. Some will recall being given a few words to learn each week and being tested at the end of the week. The words they were given were likely to have been from a spelling list in which the words are grouped according to spelling pattern. Since there can be a wide range of spelling attainment in most classes, groups within the class are likely to need words at different levels of difficulty. A disadvantage of using word lists is that words may be unrelated to ongoing work and may therefore not be practised and revised. Using words related to a topic may be more relevant and useful. Particularly in older age groups, it is best to individualize spelling by requiring the learning of words which have been misspelt in written work.

The second feature of adults' recollection of spelling in school is that they don't seem to recall being given a method for learning words. Left to themselves children will look at the word, perhaps say the letters in sequence, perhaps omitting the important stage of writing the word from memory. Spelling is, after all, for the majority of purposes a writing activity.

Poor spellers in particular should be given a procedure consisting of several steps for learning a word. The following provide for (i) a careful scrutiny of the word; (ii) trial recall; (iii) consolidation and revision.

(i)   The pupil should be encouraged to make a careful visual study of the word to note its appearance and constituent letters; to sound it slowly or pronounce it in syllables to promote attention to sound–symbol associations. With cases of severe spelling disability, the Fernald Kinaesthetic method of tracing over the word (Fernald, 1943) with a finger or pencil may be included, in order to use the kinaesthetic memories of movement in tracing it and to practise the sequence of writing movements. Some writers recommend closing the eyes and imagining the word.

(ii) The next step is *trial recall*, i.e. cover the word and try writing it without reference to the copy. (Copying may become simply a process of reproducing the word letter by letter whereas the aim is to ensure a whole reproduction in the correct sequence.) If the result is not correct, the process of scrutinizing the word and trial recall can be repeated until the word is correct.

(iii) Spelling, like rote learning of number facts, forming letters in writing and many motor skills, needs to be taken to the point where the correct response is automatic, i.e. it needs to be more than learnt; it needs to be *over-learnt*. This is a point at which much learning of spelling breaks down since it is not easy to arrange for effective revision and to ensure frequent use of words, especially in remedial teaching situations. But at least the word can be added to the pupil's own wordbook and, in cases of weak spellers, some plan of revision can be arranged.

With only slightly retarded spellers, the above process can be brief. When a correct spelling has been obtained for some written work, it may be sufficient to ensure that the word is really looked at carefully, rather than simply copied. With more seriously backward pupils, the steps in the method can be more carefully insisted upon.

A number of general points should be observed. Weak spellers should be encouraged to ask for or to find the correct spelling rather than make an attempt which may set up the wrong pattern. The word should be given in written form not aurally. Training in using a dictionary should be started as soon as feasible. Wherever possible spelling should be *writing* the spelling. Attempting to spell out the letters orally and spelling bees may be suitable for good spellers but for weak spellers it introduces a quite unnecessary difficulty – their task is simply to learn to produce the word in *writing*. There is, however, much to be said for various spelling games which both introduce an element of enjoyment and encourage attention to the details of words – Lexicon, Scrabble, crosswords, word games. Many useful suggestions are given by Hildreth (1955). Due attention and regard for good spelling can be unobtrusively developed by a combination of well-motivated practice in writing, awareness of the desirability of getting the correct spelling from some source (teacher, word list, or dictionary), adequate practice in reading and word study, and a method for promoting the correct learning of words: look, cover, write, check. The process of *looking* is helped by activities which direct pupils' attention to common letter sequences or spelling patterns in words. This structures the perception of the word as it is scrutinized. The process of *covering* the word emphasizes visualizing it in memory rather than allowing it 'to go in at one eye and out at another' (to modify a common saying). *Writing* (not copying) the word is a further step in fixing the memory of the word and the writing of it gets it on to 'the tips of the fingers' as Peters (1979) has put it.

Teaching common prefixes, suffixes and roots is one way of assisting the scrutiny of words at suitable age and reading attainment levels. Dixon (1976) developed a systematic approach known as Morphographic Spelling in which words are analysed into meaningful units (e.g. port, able, er, re, ex, de, ing; cover, un, dis, ed) and combined according to rules. The programme is published as a kit by Science Research Associates and is applicable to older primary and to secondary children.

With older and intelligent pupils, there is some place for introducing some of the commoner spelling rules which can be studied with examples. A list of rules and their limitations is given in *Studies in Spelling* (Scottish Council for Research in Education, 1961).

Handwriting difficulties

Occasionally one encounters educationally retarded pupils whose handwriting is quite reasonable – even good; they may be able to copy from the blackboard or a book in an acceptable style even though they cannot read what they have written! Much more frequently, poor readers have poor handwriting showing odd ways of forming and joining letters, sometimes with capital letters interspersed with lower case letters. Their work may make them appear more 'illiterate' than they are and may unfortunately give rise to frequent complaints about their writing which is liable to make matters worse unless positive help is given to remedy the deficiencies.

There are good reasons why attention should be given to handwriting. Apart from the obvious benefits of legibility and satisfactory appearance, clear writing assists in some measure the retention and recall of words in reading and spelling through providing additional visual study of words and through the reinforcement from the 'feel' of writing them. As reading improves, a parallel improvement in writing helps a child's general classwork and may improve their morale as well as teachers' impressions of their attainment.

A first step is to observe the poor writer as they write since the sources of difficulty cannot always be identified simply by examining the written work. The writer's posture should be considered, including the position in relation to the table or desk; and the positioning of the paper. To write in a relaxed way with neither too great nor too little pressure, the pen is best held lightly, about an inch from the point, between the thumb and first finger with the middle finger giving support. The pen should start at about 45 degrees and point towards the right of the shoulder. (For left-handers see below.)

Observation as the pupil writes will reveal instances where the direction of forming certain letters (e.g. clockwise or anti-clockwise) is incorrect or methods of joining are inappropriate. Books on handwriting (listed in further reading, p. 139) indicate groups or families of letters which can be the basis for exercises and patterns. Charts in which the starting point and direction of the writing movement are indicated by arrows might be available.

It is a matter of judging individual difficulties and needs in deciding how to tackle writing which is too large or variable in size or with ascenders and descenders too short or long. Some pupils, especially younger ones, need practice in writing without the constraint of lines. Others will be helped in remedial practice by lined paper and in some cases with lines to indicate the height of letters and perhaps also of ascenders and descenders.

Writing practice can be a dull activity and, as everyone knows, trying to retrain a faulty movement skill can be frustrating whether in playing tennis, a musical instrument or in handwriting. An atmosphere of encouragement together with reasonable explanations of why certain ways of forming or joining letters are more effective, more legible and look better should help to create a positive attitude to the task. More tangible rewards may be appropriate for some children. For some classes and age groups, a focus on handwriting might be put in a context of studying the history of writing and its different forms across the world. Occasions for 'best writing' for particular purposes such as displays should be engineered.

There are of course a variety of factors which in combination can contribute to poor handwriting. Children who are delayed in learning to read are likely to miss the practice which most children get through free writing from the infant stage onwards. And although regular handwriting practice is given throughout the primary school, it does not follow that all teachers are well versed in the recognition of difficulties and how they might be remedied. Children who have had changes of school may be confused by different writing methods. Children vary in their ability to combine a visual analysis of letter shapes with the co-ordination of appropriate movements in reproducing them. There are indeed some children (perhaps 6 per cent drawn from the whole ability range) who have a marked difficulty in visuo-motor tasks. Some children with a severe reading retardation have a disability in writing which contrasts with their general level of intellectual ability. Anderson (1976) has explained the handwriting difficulties which are quite frequent in children with spina bifida – often a source of frustration and difficulty to them. They need carefully planned, systematic help as well as encouragement.

The left-handed writer

Many left-handers have no special difficulty in writing but teachers need to be aware of certain considerations. Writing with the left hand is different from writing with the right. The natural and easier movement is away from the body but the left-hander has to move their arm in towards the body with the likelihood of constricted movement as they get to the end of the line. The position of the pen on upward strokes makes scratching the paper more likely. Some left-handers adopt a crook position with the hand pointing back towards the body. Occasionally there is a tendency to mirror-write.

The left-hander needs to be taught how to write left-handedly and certain differences of procedure which help them should be known by all teachers, since left-handed writing occurs in 8 per cent of the school population (Clark, 1974).

1. *Position.* To prepare for the inward movement of the arm to the body, the child should sit slightly to the right of the desk with the book towards the left. The child has freedom of movement throughout a line of writing.
2. *The paper* should be tilted slightly so that the bottom right corner is nearer to the body. This allows the child to see what they are writing, avoids smudging, eliminates the need for any tendency to a hook position of the wrist and hand, and puts the pen in a better position for writing vertically or with a forward slope.
3. *The pen* should point towards the left shoulder. Fine nibs should be avoided since they are more likely to dig into the

paper. A broad flexible nib is required. Nibs with a slanting tip specially designed for left-handers are available. There are several cheap but reliable fountain pens with replaceable nibs which provide for this.
4. *Grip of the pen.* It should not be held too near the nib, so that the line of writing can be seen.

The recommendations about teaching handwriting apply with greater force to left-handers: a relaxed hold on the pen, starting with large movements, learning efficient ways of writing letters. Allowance for slower writing in left-handers should also be made. They may well need help in acquiring and maintaining left-to-right movements and avoiding reversals. A child who mirror writes can be helped to start at the left by writing from a ruled margin.

Mathematics

Considering the amount of time and effort expended by teachers in teaching mathematics in school, it is a little surprising that until recently there have been rather few attempts to find out what use is made of mathematics in adult life. An American study made by Wilson (1919) is often quoted. Of the social and business problems solved by over 4,000 adults during a two-week period, 83 per cent involved buying and selling goods, 11 per cent involved money but not buying and selling, and 6 per cent required measures. Most of the processes were addition and multiplication, common fractions, making out and understanding accounts. Another American study by Peterson (1972) drew information from 70 teachers over a ten-day period. They recorded bills, purchases, measuring in cooking and sewing, wages, tax, weighing on bathroom scales, dialling telephone, setting the dial on the refrigerator, addressing letters.

In England, Moore (1957) decided to follow Wilson's inquiry in order to identify priorities in revising the mathematics syllabus in a special school for 'educationally subnormal children'. A record was kept by 88 adults for a week. Of the 2,837 problems recorded, 1,512 had to do with money. 291 of these required addition and subtraction, performed mentally. Other number problems were mostly addition, with some subtraction and multiplication but little division. Only 6 per cent of problems involved capacity, linear measurement and fractions (halves, quarters, eighths).

Thompson (1962) was concerned with 'educationally subnormal children' about to leave or having left school. He found that 88 per cent of their uses of mathematics were concerned with money. Problems were mostly oral except for some simple budgeting and completing time sheets. There was some need to read and understand numbers and some use of counting and addition, measuring, telling time and reading timetables. The language of number was often required. Rent, rates, insurance and hire purchase were encountered without being well understood.

Findings such as these have had some influence in identifying priorities for leavers' programmes in special schools but their overall significance for the mathematics curriculum for low attainers should not be overestimated. A Schools Council working paper (Denvir *et al.*, 1982) on policies and practices suggested that in addition to the usefulness of mathematics in everyday living and in work, it is also part of our culture of which all children should have experience and is or should be pleasurable – a potential source of enjoyment. The latter is obviously important with low attainers whose limited skills and understanding in mathematics (in spite sometimes of greater achievements in other subjects) can result in a limited range and repetitive experience of mathematics. To these three, we should add the importance of mathematics for cognitive development, i.e. the development of concepts and thinking processes – those such as classification and ordering which are part of the process of making sense of our experience and those such as problem solving which even in the simple affairs of living enable us to respond to variable situations.

A rather broader view of mathematics in the lives of adults was obtained in an inquiry commissioned by the Cockcroft Committee of Inquiry into the teaching of mathematics in schools (DES, 1982). Interviews were carried out sensitively with about 100 adults to explore by discussion their mathematical usage and by presenting them with real life situations (Sewell, 1980). The researcher's first problem was to obtain her sample: 'there was a widespread reluctance to be interviewed about mathematics' even if the dreaded word was replaced by 'arithmetic' or 'everyday use of numbers'. Half the people initially approached refused to participate! The Cockcroft Committee commented that perhaps the most striking feature of the study was the extent to which a simple piece of mathematics could induce feelings of anxiety, helplessness, fear and even guilt – often in people who were otherwise competent and even well-qualified in other fields.

Some particular findings were that people often lacked the confidence to try alternative methods of solving simple practical problems and quite often felt inadequate because they were not using 'the proper method'. There was a widespread inability to understand percentages; difficulty was shown in reading charts and timetables. Many strategies were used to cope with mathematical demands of adult life such as always buying £10 of petrol, paying by cheque and taking more money than likely to be needed to pay bills at checkouts because of uncertainty about the total of purchases being made. Some relied on husbands, wives or children to check and pay bills.

The Cockcroft Committee concluded that they would include the following among the mathematical needs of adult life: the ability to read numbers and count; to tell the time; to pay for purchases; to weigh and measure; to understand timetables, graphs and charts; and to carry out any necessary calculations. They recognized that some people would achieve much more than this because of their needs at work. The committee also referred to the importance of a feeling for number which permitted sensible estimation and approximation, e.g. realizing that three items at 95p will be a little less than £3.

Parallel inquiries into the use of mathematics in employment provided interesting findings which are available in a number of reports and papers referred to at the end of this chapter. For our purpose, we may note that knowledge of calculations learnt at school had often atrophied, that employees who were required to use particular ones regularly became quite proficient with practice. There were often particular methods in use as well as calculators and other forms of reckoning which gave assistance.

The report underlined the importance of confidence in making effective use of mathematical skills and knowledge, whether this is little or much. In a discussion of the concept of numeracy, the committee specified, first, an 'at homeness' with number which enables individuals to cope with practical everyday demands and, secondly, the ability to understand information presented in graphs, charts, tables of percentages.

The achievement of understanding and a sense of 'at homeness' have been among the aims of developments in the mathematics curriculum and teaching methods in the last decade or so. Some of these such as the Mathematics for the Majority Continuation Project aimed to avoid mathematics which has been described as 'a mysterious, solemn ritual at best, and at worst... a dose of rather nasty medicine to be taken at regular intervals' and to provide thematic materials on topics such as athletics, aircraft, buildings, fashion, holidays, communication. One school pointed out that the topic work occupied two-fifths of the available mathematics time and that in the remainder the attempt was made to develop relevant skills more systematically. Cawley (1976) has also made a case for 'social arithmetic' with slow learners. He suggests that teachers often feel guilty about social topics but argues that 'The topics are not intended to sugar the pill of computation. Because this is the way mathematical skills can be used in everyday life, they are the medicine itself.' Making an analogy between computation skills in mathematics and phonic skills in reading, he suggests that written computation without reference to real situations is like phonics practice without reference to words and sentences. He suggests that we should do what we do with writing and sometimes with reading – employ reality as near as we can to the classroom, check pupils' understanding of situations, extend understanding by exploring the relationships and finally develop increasing precision. Specific help with skills can be given as the need arises – as indeed they are in English. The writer outlines topics and activities under such headings as the School Community, Shopping, Travel, Sport and Leisure.

This point of view was echoed in articles by Fitzgerald (1984) reporting observations of the use of mathematics in employment. He concludes that schools cannot easily simulate the job contexts in which employees carry out mathematical tasks although pupils' interest can be stimulated by adapting in the classroom examples from employment. However, he envisages the linking of the subject more closely to extended practical activities undertaken by pupils and gives examples such as designing and constructing of models, ornaments, musical instruments, clothes, boats, hi-fi equipment, computers, horticultural experiments, orienteering, etc., together with consideration of financial transactions. At least pupils could be applying mathematics in meaningful contexts and might develop more positive attitudes toward the subject.

Sources of difficulty

The adults interviewed by Sewell who had difficulties in mathematics often attributed their failure and dislike of the subject to some specific cause when young – changes of teacher or school; absences through illness; being promoted to a higher class and falling behind; an unsympathetic teacher; over expectation, especially by fathers. The list illustrates two important features of learning mathematics. It is a subject in which learning is sequential and any discontinuity is liable to affect progress. Later concepts and topics depend upon previous ones. For example, uncertain understanding of the relationship between numbers to ten will affect learning beyond ten. A poor grasp of numbers to 100 will affect work in money, the metric system and percentages. A failure to appreciate fully the relationship between arithmetical processes such as addition, subtraction, multiplication and division will affect many everyday computations as well as higher levels of mathematics. Weaknesses in the structure of understanding may easily go unrecognized unless revealed by observation and discussion with individuals as they try to solve problems.

The list also indicates the emotional factors in learning. Apart from those mentioned, it has been suggested that the 'either right or wrong' nature of mathematics contributes to lack of confidence in some children. There is no doubt too that maths requires a more directed effort which is more difficult for some than others, perhaps because of its apparent remoteness from real things, perhaps because the individual has more compelling interests and satisfactions, perhaps because of other personality traits. Schonell suggested that among children with difficulties one finds some who are impulsive, quick and careless of detail. Where failure sets in, there are likely to be negative attitudes. The issue of motivation is obviously important and a continuing concern is how to establish and maintain a sense of success and achievement.

An aspect which needs to be considered, especially in teaching low attainers, is the effect of experience at different ages and levels. In the infant school, children who have had pre-mathematics experience in the nursery school or through a variety of play materials at home are better prepared for activities in school. They are also more likely to have acquired some of the vocabulary and the language forms which the teacher uses and prompts children to use. The background of experience continues to have an influence through the school years, progress depending to some degree on the practical activities and language obtained through play materials, hobbies, models, construction sets and games of various kinds. Supportive experiences may be limited in some homes and the interests of some families may tend to the verbal/aesthetic rather than the mathematical/scientific.

Mathematics learning itself presents difficulties because, while it is a way of dealing with real things, it involves abstractions and relationships derived from activity and experience. The ability to develop concepts and perceive relationships partly depends on children's mental development, though mathematics teaching itself must be seen as one of the ways in which schooling helps to develop intelligence. Matching teaching to children's concept development and trying to ensure understanding as well as skills and competence are not simple. Some of the chief tasks of primary mathematics are to teach concepts of numbers and the way numerals are used to symbolize numbers; an understanding of operations (addition, subtractio.1, multiplication and division); and discovering relationships between numbers. Apart from the symbols, all these are ideas which grow out of thinking about actions with materials. Numbers, operations and relationships are abstractions from experiences of grouping, manipulating and comparing things. Mathematical symbols are a convenient way of making statements about these abstractions, and just as young children sometimes pick up words and expressions about which they have no comprehension, so it is quite possible for mathematical symbols to be used with no real understanding, or only with partial understanding.

It is only too easy, for example, for children to work through well-graded series of sums and to be quite proficient at making the right response within the range of numbers and operations which are being practised at a particular time. Yet the teacher may be baffled by the inability of some children to give sensible answers to the same tasks orally or to use apparently learnt facts in everyday problems. What can be even more baffling is that this can occur even when children have had ample experience with apparatus prior to meeting the tasks in symbolic form. They have not abstracted the ideas from their concrete experiences, or the ideas are not sufficiently grasped to be thought about without concrete aids.

Similar difficulties occur at further stages of primary mathematics. It is not uncommon for children to treat signs (+, −, etc.) in a confused fashion and while this may be due to carelessness it is sometimes due to an imperfect grasp of the meaning of the operations and their relatedness, which is further demonstrated by difficulty in identifying what mathematical operation is required in a verbal problem. Another common type of difficulty, such as dealing with place value in written work, may result from an inadequate understanding from practical experiences of how the number system is based on ten, as well as failure to understand how place value is used to symbolize this. While verbal explanations alone may be sufficient to correct some misconceptions, it is frequently necessary to go back to concrete experiences in order to reconstruct the necessary concepts.

The work of Piaget has been a major influence in directing attention to the fact that reasoning processes develop out of activity. To take a simple example, the concept of putting objects in a series according to size seems so obvious to adults that it is easy to underestimate its difficulty for a young child. Pre-school children can say which of two rods is longer. It is not until the infant stage that children can place several things into a series. The children's difficulty is that instead of having to find one relationship they have to combine two relationships – the rod is both smaller than the next and bigger than the previous one – and they also have to co-ordinate a series of such relationships. Through many experiences of making and co-ordinating judgements of this kind as they seriate different materials, the children gradually construct a mental schema of a series which helps them to anticipate and guide their actions. This mental schema or concept becomes a mental tool which they can apply to other things in their environment. Moreover, they can perform the operation quickly without going through all the detailed comparisons they did when they were learning it.

The possibility should be borne in mind, especially with slow learners or handicapped children, that some children may have marked disabilities in some of the perceptual and thinking processes involved in the transition from action to thought just described. For example, children who have difficulty in organizing their visuo-spatial perception may have difficulty in distinguishing quickly differences in shapes, sizes, amounts and length. They cannot look at groups of objects or at number rods and tell which contains the greatest amount. Some have difficulty in estimating distances and dealing with shapes and patterns. Johnson and Myklebust (1967) claim that these children have rarely enjoyed working with puzzles, models or constructional toys. Certainly, some cerebral-palsied children with marked spatial difficulties are very weak in number concepts, and it is also interesting that the children with visuo-motor difficulties whom Brenner described (p. 49) tended to be good at reading but poor in mathematics. But in general children with marked lack of 'number sense' do not seem to have been studied very much.

The schema of ordering things or groups in a succession underlies much of primary mathematics. Later two series can be related and represented pictorially or graphically, building up an understanding which has many instances in the secondary curriculum and adult life. The adults who claimed not to understand graphs may not have experienced, or not fully grasped, some of the work which is now commonly undertaken in schools. Likewise adults who said they were confused about percentages were probably taught to work out percentages by a procedure which they did not have insight into. The recommendation in the Cockcroft Committee's foundation list of topics that the teaching of percentages should be based on the idea that 1 per cent means '1p in every pound' or 'one in every hundred' is an example of linking a concept to an existing schema.

On the same theme, Skemp (1971) distinguished between relational understanding and instrumental understanding. The former refers to knowing what to do and why, the latter refers to knowing what to do by rote or rules. Relational understanding develops plans or schemas which can be widely used rather than limited to set tasks and procedures.

'Knowing why' does not mean that the child can verbalize it efficiently, though they may do. We often perform actions appropriately and effectively but would find it harder to express why or how. However, in mathematics learning language is an important guide to activity and a means of thinking and communicating about it. The vocabulary of primary mathematics is extensive and can also be confusing so that every school should have a policy about the language to be used and how it is to be extended during the age groups. Slow learners are very likely to have more limited vocabulary and less confidence in expressing ideas; they may have more difficulty in comprehending the teacher's language forms.

Beyond that, there is the need to develop an understanding of symbols, so familiar and easy for the adult but for the child a further step from the real things and structural apparatus through which their understanding of concepts and relationships have been developing. Pinfield (1982) comments that children have been using language for three or four years before they are introduced to the symbols of reading yet the interval between experience and symbols in mathematics is far shorter. The school age child is perhaps intellectually more able to cope with that but the point is a very appropriate one in respect of less intelligent children.

In addition to a relational understanding of the number system, there are other concepts to be constructed from activity and experience: for example, linear measurement and weight each with their associated language requirements and needs for integration with other schemas, for example, number and operations. As classes progress through the age groups, it is not difficult to appreciate that slower children can be introduced prematurely to new stages.

In general, they tend to be poor in memory processes, in retaining learning even after frequent practice and revision. It can be difficult to monitor their progress. Some schools, particularly special schools, have reported positively about more systematic methods of teaching to specific objectives, with frequent and brief checks. Some schools have reported successful experience with direct instructional methods such as DISTAR (Direct Instructional Systems to Arithmetic and Reading).

At the beginning of the secondary stage, most schools undertake assessment of attainments. Bailey (1982) suggests distinguishing three groups, the first with mathematics attainment below the seven-year level, the second between 7 and 11 and the third from 11 upwards.

The first group is likely to be small unless a special school or class is transferring pupils to mainstream at 11. Pupils at this level need individual study including information from primary school records to establish what understanding they have of number, measure, money, time-telling and the language of mathematics. They – as well as some in Group B – need a continuation of a primary school approach using materials such as Cuisenaire rods or other structural apparatus.

Those in the second group will show a variety of deficiencies and levels which can be explored by the use of a criterion referenced checklist such as Yardsticks (see further reading, p. 139) as well as by observation of performance and discussion aiming to obtain an impression of misunderstanding of processes, confusion about signs, place value, and difficulty in using number in simple oral problems. Poor reading attainment will be noted for its relevance to the use of books and workcards. *Ways and Means 2* (Taylor, 1981) contains appraisals of teaching materials and mathematics books for pupils with learning difficulties.

For pupils at this level, there is the danger that the work they need may simply be seen as a continuation of their primary school work. The Cockcroft Committee made a number of pertinent comments on provision for pupils whose attainment is low. In particular, they indicate: the need for the mathematics department to be involved in teaching at this level since remedial teachers are often less confident about the teaching of mathematics and the syllabus can sometimes be excessively narrow; the need for ample opportunity for oral work and discussion: 'mathematics should not be regarded as something pupils can get on with by themselves while the teacher is hearing other pupils read.' A new element in the content or teaching approach might be sought to encourage them to make a fresh start and to believe that they are making progress. A well-planned progression using a behavioural objectives approach (Ainscow and Tweddle) might be considered or employing precision teaching in which within graded practice there are daily checks on correctness and rate of performance which can be charted to provide teacher and pupil knowledge of progress. Topic work and interesting activity of inquiry should be an element in their programme. Encouragement and a motivating atmosphere are obviously crucial if they are to progress. A convenient source of reference for the range of primary work which will not have been completed by those pupils is in Duncan's book on *Mathematics for Slow Learners* (1978) and numerous articles in *Remedial Education* and *Mathematics in School* over recent years describe the ways in which teachers have tried to maintain interest and progress.

For later age groups, the Schools Council study of low attainers refers to schools replacing a sequential approach by self-contained topics and in some cases by individualized programmes. A mathematics element is likely to be found within special courses arranged for those not following examinations and the final years provide opportunities for mathematics in relation to post-school needs – dealing with money transactions, budgets, holidays, leisure, travel, wages and benefits, use of calculators, computers. The Cockcroft Report on Mathematics in Schools (1982) set out a foundation list of mathematics topics which should form part of the mathematics syllabus for pupils in about the lowest 40 per cent in the range of attainment in mathematics (paras. 455-466). This list together with its annotated comments, based partly on the findings of inquiries into the mathematical needs of adult life and in employment, should be familiar to all teachers, not only mathematicians, since opportunities for using mathematical topics occurs in many aspects of the curriculum.

List of further reading

Reading
HUTCHCROFT, D.M.R. (1981). *Making Language Work*. London: McGraw Hill.
MOON, C. and RABAN, B. (1975). *A Question of Reading*. Basingstoke: Macmillan Educational.
SMITH, F. (1978). *Reading*. Cambridge: Cambridge University Press.
WESTWOOD, P.S. (1975). *The Remedial Teachers' Handbook*. Edinburgh: Oliver and Boyd.

Spelling
DIXON, R. (1976). *Morphographic Spelling*. Henley-on-Thames: Science Research Associates.
PETERS, M.L. (1967). *Spelling – Caught or Taught?* London: Routledge and Kegan Paul.
TODD, J. (1982). *Learning to Spell*. Oxford: Blackwell.
TORBE, M. (1978). *Teaching Spelling*. London: Ward Lock.

Handwriting
INGLIS, A. and CONNELL, E. (1964). *The Teaching of Handwriting*. Walton-on-Thames: Nelson.
JARMAN, C. (1979). *The Development of Handwriting Skills*. Oxford: Blackwell.
PHILLIPS, R.C. (1976). *The Skills of Handwriting*. Oxford: R.C. Phillips.

SASSOON, R. (1983). *Practical Guide to Children's Handwriting*. London: Thames and Hudson.

SMITH, P. (1977). *Developing Handwriting*. London: Macmillan Educational.

Mathematics

DENVIR, B., STOLZ, C. and BROWN, M. (1982). *Low Attainers in Mathematics 5–16*. Schools Council Working Paper 72. London: Methuen Educational

EDWARDS, R. (1978). 'Mathematics 14–16'. In: HINSON, M. (Ed) *Encouraging Results*. London: Macdonald Educational.

GREAT BRITAIN. DEPARTMENT OF EDUCATION AND SCIENCE (1982). *Mathematics Counts* (The Cockcroft Report). Especially 334–338, 455–458, 459–469. London: HMSO.

PINFIELD, B. (1982). 'Mathematics for primary school children with learning difficulties'. In: HINSON, M. and HUGHES, M. (Eds) *Planning Effective Progress*. London: Hulton Educational.

WILLIAMS, A.A. (1985). 'Towards success in mathematics'. In: SMITH, C.J. (Ed) *New Directions in Remedial Education*. Lewes: The Falmer Press.

YARDSTICKS.   Criterion-referenced   test   in   mathematics. Walton-on-Thames: Nelson.

CHAPTER 7
Further Education and Vocational Preparation

The majority of pupils have always left school at the age marking the end of compulsory education and until recent times went straight into work. The advantage – and for some families the necessity – of having another wage earner was an important consideration, coupled perhaps with a limited view of schooling as something that had to be gone through before starting the real business of working and living. Some leavers taking up occupations requiring particular knowledge, skills and qualifications attended technical and further education colleges for evening classes or day-release classes. For those with learning difficulties – who might be thought to have as much need as others for continuing their education – there has been little provision until recently, other than basic literacy classes.

The need for post-16 education and training

Future generations may be as much surprised that the majority ended their formal education at 16 as we are that children earlier in this century could leave school at 13. We are moving into an era when there is recognition of the need for further education and vocational preparation for all young people and indeed for continuing education in adult life in order to enrich the quality of life as well as to keep abreast of new developments in jobs and careers and in some cases to retrain.

The case for further education for all young people – not just the academically and vocationally inclined – has many facets. For a start, we no longer accept that mental and educational abilities reach a ceiling in adolescence; we know that abilities and capacities continue to develop through further educational experience, particularly when motivation is heightened by its relevance to work and life. Moreover, late adolescence is a formative period which needs both the stimulus and freedom of wider experience and a continuing framework of support within the family, education and vocational preparation. It is a formative period for personal development – discovering the sort of person one is, would like to be and could be – and also for becoming a member of society – developing social skills, attitudes and values. Adolescence is a critical period in any society at any period of time; in the present, the demands of living and working in an increasingly complex society call for higher levels of skill and adaptability. Since a smaller proportion of people's lives than formerly are likely to be spent in paid employment, education must be concerned with developing people's personal resources as well as vocational potentialities. The creation of a coherent and balanced form of education and training for all young people from 16 to 19 is thus one of the most important and exciting challenges at the present time.

It is not difficult to accept that all this applies with even greater force to young people with special needs. Those with physical and sensory disabilities may need special provisions in order to improve their chances of participating as fully as possible in work and social life. Those with limited attainments and personal immaturities need a longer period than at present to develop their potentialities, independence and self-reliance; in doing so, in the different setting of further education they sometimes discover previously unrecognized interests and capacities. For many young people with special needs, further education gives them much needed experience of mixing with others and joining in the activities and interests of their age group. Anderson and Clarke (1982) have shown how those with physical disabilities are often lonely, bored and depressed partly as a consequence of mobility and transport problems. Less able and educationally retarded young people may also have such difficulties as a result of immaturities, lack of interests, lack of work and social opportunities. In a period of high youth unemployment, these social as well as educational needs deserve particular attention.

It is not surprising that the Warnock Committee identified provision for young people over 16 with special educational needs as one of its three areas of main priority. The report mentioned in particular the importance of a reassessment of their needs with future prospects in mind two years before leaving school; the importance of careers guidance in school and of the work of specialist careers officers; preparation at school for the transition to adult life; opportunities to continue their education at school or in further education and for suitable courses of vocational preparation; the need for experienced staff to give support in the post-16 period in schools and colleges.

Preparation in schools

Teachers of children with learning difficulties have always shown concern for the post-school progress of pupils. In special schools particularly, efforts have been made to maintain contact with pupils, sometimes by means of a youth club or literacy class in order to give some continuing support. There have been many follow-up studies of the progress of leavers from special schools for pupils with moderate learning difficulties (summaries are given in Brennan, 1974, Chap. 4) and a few follow-up studies have been carried out over several decades (Atkinson, 1984). These commonly show that, in periods when there is a normal level of employment, some three-quarters of these ex-pupils have obtained jobs and settled reasonably well into adult life. A great variety of factors contribute to less satisfactory adjustment – very low ability, additional disabilities, personality characteristics leading to difficulties in employment, lack of support from families and other sources.

Teachers' awareness of the difficulties of transition to post-school life led to the development of leavers' programmes in the final two years of school. Preparation for employment by means of visits to different places of work, the involvement of the careers officer, work experience within the school and in local firms enabled pupils to see the relevance of literacy and numeracy, money, time, measurement, independence in travel, shopping, form filling, applying for jobs, interviews, telephoning, social security and other agencies. Preparation for broader aspects of living involved communication and social skills, home management, parenthood, health and sex education, leisure. Special schools have often been able to accommodate leavers in a separate area of the school and to give them more independence and responsibility. Frequently, leavers have been able to attend a local college of further education on a link course for one or two days a week in which they sample a variety of courses with the aim of developing interests and finding aptitudes relevant to job placement or later further education.

Successful as such courses have proved, teachers have always been aware that some pupils were still too immature in their personal and general competence and that ideally they needed a longer period at school. A few, where parents were willing, were able to stay longer at school; some were placed for a three-month course of assessment and training at an employment rehabilitation centre (run by the Manpower Services Commission). Jerrold and Fox (1968) described a workshop set up adjacent to their special school where a number of pupils stayed on for a year's preparation in a realistic work setting. Browne (1979) has described an industrial unit at Bridgend with a similar purpose.

Further education provision

A few colleges of further education pioneered full-time courses for young people with special needs but a survey in 1969–70 undertaken by the National Children's Bureau showed that there were too few opportunities and that they were unevenly provided across the handicaps (Tuckey *et al.*, 1973). Only 37 per cent of 788 handicapped young people had entered some form of further education or training. In fact, only 20 per cent went into higher or further education or to special colleges for the handicapped. Most of these were either visually handicapped for whom there are long-established colleges or were physically handicapped for whom there are a number of special residential colleges. Only 2 per cent of those with moderate learning difficulties and 10 per cent of the whole sample had gone on to a college of further education.

During the 1970s a number of trends resulted in more provision in colleges of further education. First, the scope of further education courses in colleges widened as the need for some of their traditional work declined (such as day-release courses for apprentices). In addition to a broader range of courses leading to academic and vocational qualifications, there was increasing recognition of the needs of young people with learning difficulties and other special needs – often a response to the concern of schools and the careers service. Another factor was government concern about training for employment. In 1973, the Manpower Services Commission was established to take responsibility for, and to improve, industrial and commercial training. The Training Opportunities Scheme (TOPS) was available for retraining adults and some courses were available in colleges and adult education centres for those with limited social and educational attainments. From 1975, the Commission's attention turned to leavers in the transition from school to work and in 1978, in the face of rising unemployment, the Youth Opportunities Programme (YOP) was initiated to provide work preparation courses in skill centres and colleges (20 per cent of the intake to the YOP scheme) and work experience on employers' premises (80 per cent). Colleges of further education were involved in educational support for young people on work experience placements and in providing Work Introduction Courses (WICs). These aimed to provide less able young people from special and comprehensive schools with a range of work skills as well as education in life and social skills relevant to the world of work. Bradley and Hegarty (1982) quote a course offering the following modules: woodwork, metalwork, building, office duties; display, decoration and design; food preparation; life-skills, including basic literacy, numeracy, etc.; work experience. The aim was to develop skills relevant to employment by teaching the use of tools and procedures. The educational component in WIC courses was required to be relevant to work. In a survey of 32 WIC courses, McDaid (1982) found students generally positive to the experience, expecially the work aspect, less so to life-skills because it often involved writing. She found that many staff involved were not experienced or trained for teaching the less able; the need for in-service training of lecturers was apparent. The courses were usually of 13 weeks' duration and at most 26 weeks. That this was too short a time was soon recognized as well as the lack of any guarantee of employment. The implementation of a Youth Training Scheme (YTS) began in

September 1983. It was designed to provide opportunities lasting a whole year for all 16-year-olds who had left full-time education and were unemployed; its local delivery was delegated to 'managing agents' – local authorities, voluntary organizations, large employers.

One can point to many deficiencies in these developments – the short duration of the YOP courses and even the 12 months of the YTS; the need to develop training of staff in the needs of the less able in further education (in-service training of staff is currently the subject of an inquiry by the Bureau for Handicapped Students); and of course there is the backdrop of high youth unemployment. Nevertheless, what has been developing is a curriculum for the average and below average post-16-year-old which as Baillie (1982) pointed out 'owes little or nothing to the academic or subject based curriculum'. If anything, as he says, the practical basis has great similarities with the preoccupations of teachers in special schools – whose leavers' programmes were referred to earlier. It is a curriculum which has relevance through being based on direct experience of work and other real-life situations: the acquisition of relevant basic skills and knowledge; the development of self-knowledge and personal responsibility, assisted by counselling, guidance and assessment. It is a curriculum appropriate to less academic students staying on in the VI forms of ordinary schools or moving into colleges of further education.

A significant influence in the development of this curriculum conception was the work of the Further Education Curriculum Review and Development Unit (FEU) established by the DES to assist further education staff engaged in vocational preparation. From 1978, a number of reports on curriculum and assessment have made valuable contributions to the process of defining the objectives and structure of courses as well as methods of assessment. Of particular note was *A Basis for Choice* (FEU, 1979; revised 1982), the report of a study group on full-time courses for leavers requiring something other than GCE studies or courses for specific occupations. It described a curriculum of vocational preparation which had three elements: a common core of vocational and social skills for 50 to 60 per cent of the time, with half of the remaining time for vocational studies for a general area of employment and half to job specific studies. It aimed to define a curriculum which would be educationally sound in that it provided young people with learning experiences through which they would extend their understanding of their roles as members of society and in the world of work; would develop their mental, physical and educational skills; their ability to develop satisfactory personal relationships; their everyday coping skills; adaptability; and a basis for realistic decisions about their future. This publication also offers methods of assessing students' progress by means of profiles in which levels of achievement in attainments in the common core are specified and which would be readily interpreted by employers and others. It is a curriculum which recognizes young people's need for learning which is rather different in content and mode from school learning and which draws upon their motivation to move into the adult world.

Another publication *Beyond coping: some approaches to social education* (FEU, 1980) examines the meaning of such terms as social skills, life-skills, social education and also examines the different types of approach to social education.

Skills for Living is an account of an attempt to develop a curriculum for students with moderate learning difficulties from five aims important in their further education: essentially, understanding themselves and society; leisure and work; getting on with people and presenting themselves well; being responsible; staying solvent and coping in normal circumstances. It is not intended to be prescriptive but to suggest a pattern for curriculum development in this area.

Special courses and units

Bradley and Hegarty's (1982) survey of further education for students with special needs details a number of special courses (six months or one year) run by colleges either without, or partially with, MSC support. Courses are for students with moderate learning difficulties (the most common) and cover in various patterns the content of work preparation, social and life skills, basic educational skills and work experience referred to earlier. One such course for students with moderate learning difficulties from special and comprehensive schools is offered by a sixth-form college and includes life-skills (earning a living, living with others, setting up home, going places, living with leisure), basic skills – literacy, numeracy, technology and simple computer work; counselling; general studies and physical activities – which are taken in mixed groups of other students. Mention should also be made of one- and two-year full-time courses for students with severe learning difficulties which currently number between 20 and 30. Students are integrated in some practical and creative courses in colleges as well as having their own programme and participating in other ways in college activities (Aldridge, 1982; Dean and Hegarty, 1984).

At the present time, there are some dozen colleges of further education which have organized a more extensive and specialist provision for the assessment and training of young people with special needs. One of the recommendations of the Warnock Report was that there should be within each region at least one special unit providing special courses for young people with more severe disabilities or difficulties and based in an establishment of further education. They had in mind the needs of young people with sensory or physical disabilities and those with moderate or severe learning difficulties. Wherever possible of course one would hope that such young people would find a suitable course and specialist teaching and resources in a local college. But there is a case for some special units in which specialist staff have developed expertise in the assessment of the personal, social and vocational needs of students with special needs. For those with sensory disabilities, the provision of the necessary aids and technical resources; for the physically disabled and those with moderate and severe learning difficulties, medical and other forms of care, speech therapy and physiotherapy should be available. For all students with special needs, personal counselling, vocational assessment and guidance are needed. Students do not, of course, need to remain in the unit but, with support if needed, may follow appropriate courses in other departments of the college. A good example of this is the Work Orientation Unit at North Nottinghamshire College, Worksop. Its development was reported by Hutchinson and Clegg (1975) and by Hutchinson (1982). Beginning with four students in 1965, there were 147 students in 1978, about half of whom had moderate or severe learning difficulties, a quarter had physical disabilities, 18 had sensory handicaps and 15 had emotional and behaviour difficulties. The staffing consisted of 13 special education teachers and 33 technical teaching staff. Following initial assessment, there are three levels of course provision: students may be placed full-time for vocational and educational training in another department of the college but with support if required from the special unit; there may be partial placement in another department but with basic education and support in the unit; students may be full-time in the unit following specially designed courses of work experience and training in a purpose-built special training workshop, basic education courses and social/recreational courses. Attendance may be for two years or more.

This well-developed unit attracts students with special needs from a wide geographical area which illustrates both the need and the shortage, until recently at least, of suitable local provision. This is however gradually being remedied as the further education sector gears itself up to a new and challenging role.

Mention should also be made of specialist residential colleges of further education and vocational training. Those for visually handicapped and physically handicapped young people are long established and others have been established in recent years by voluntary organizations and independent groups, often offering education and training for young people with particular needs not available in their locality.

Beyond further education

There have always been some young people with marked disabilities who did not obtain employment. The high rate of unemployment affecting a large proportion of young people is increasing the number of those with special needs who fail – even after training – to get work. An issue we have to face and consider carefully is what the alternatives might be for those without work. There may be implications for education in schools and colleges and also for the development of centres in the community which reduce the isolation and boredom and in a productive way develop alternatives to work. Little has been written on this topic but a paper by Anderson and Tizard (Centre for Educational Research and Innovation, 1979; Clarke and Tizard, 1983) is a thoughtful discussion with suggested implications for education. Massie

(1982) has written a stimulating discussion of the issue.

The educator cannot ignore trends in society which may affect students' lives in the future. The teachers' role is however to educate – to develop understanding, personal resources, social and practical skills – and the recent developments in post-16 education for students with special needs are a much needed extension of what has been done in school to prepare young people for life.

List of further reading

Educare. Journal of the National Bureau of Handicapped Students.

*FURTHER EDUCATION CURRICULUM REVIEW AND DEVELOPMENT UNIT.

Making Progress (1982). A review of research and practice in the assessment of students with special needs.

Skills for Living (1982). A curriculum framework for students with moderate learning difficulties.

Stretching the System (1982). Examples of provision in further education for special needs.

Students with special needs in F.E. (1981). A review of research and developments.

Teaching & Learning Strategies for F.E. students with special needs (1983). Guidelines derived from innovative practice in colleges and workshops.

HUTCHINSON, D. (1982). *Work Preparation for the Handicapped.* London: Croom Helm.

Special Education: Forward Trends, vol. 9, no. 3. Issue on further education.

* These publications are available from Publications Despatch Centre, Honeypot Lane, Canons Park, Stanmore, Middlesex HA7 1A2.

CHAPTER 8
The Training of Teachers

The concept of special educational needs which developed during the 1970s and was the basis for legislation in the 1980s, has wide implications for the organization, curricula and teaching in schools and for teachers' co-operation with other professions and with parents. Legislation does not create a new pattern overnight; it provides a framework for a new phase of development. How well it develops depends, of course, on the availability and deployment of resources and on research which monitors new practice and charts future directions. Most important of all are teachers and schools as they try to translate ideas into practice, as they communicate and exchange their experience and push forward new developments. Many examples of innovation by teachers, schools, support services and local education authorities have been referred to in this book.

Not surprisingly, the Warnock Report identified the initial and in-service training of teachers as one of its three areas of first priority; a report of the Advisory Committee on the Supply and Education of Teachers (ACSET) confirmed and extended its recommendations.

Both reports affirmed that *all* teachers of the 2 to 19 age group should be able to identify the special educational needs of children and young people, should understand what they can do to meet their needs and how to enlist specialist advice and help. A foundation of this should be provided in initial teacher training. The Warnock Report indicated the awareness and skills which should be included in a special educational element and ACSET emphasized that the intentions cannot be achieved only by specific content on special needs but must permeate the whole course of training.

The Warnock Report recommended that serving teachers should have a comparable introduction to special educational needs and provisions – which would be a considerable undertaking. A number of packages of materials including videos has been developed and some LEAs have organized 'awareness' courses as envisaged by the Warnock Committee. The ACSET report, perhaps more realistically, identified certain priority groups for in-service courses suited to their particular needs. For example, all management courses for heads and senior staff should include elements concerned with special educational needs and the organization of resources to meet them. Another priority group would be designated teachers with responsibility for special needs and for organizing forms of help which will give such pupils access to the curriculum. The designation of such a teacher or co-ordinator in a school together with the commitment of senior staff should be key factors in the development of a whole school policy in regard to the curriculum, teaching and other forms of help for children with special needs. It implies school-based in-service training both informally as teachers seek help and advice and formally by drawing upon the expertise of support and advisory services and the School Psychological Service in school-based in-service training. In some LEAs, the co-ordinators are the focus of much of the in-service training in special needs and also are agents for the dissemination of ideas and practice.

The ACSET report went on to discuss the needs of LEAs for 'specialist teachers who between them have detailed knowledge of the spectrum of special educational needs and the responses required, whether these teachers are employed in ordinary or special schools or within a peripatetic service'. It was envisaged that such teachers would undertake a full-time or equivalent part-time course leading to a recognized qualification in special educational needs. It was stressed that such teachers should have a firm foundation of experience of teaching in ordinary schools. There are a number of reasons for this. First, we aspire to provide children with special educational needs, even those with severe and complex disabilities, as normal an educational experience as we can contrive. Secondly, the trend towards integrated forms of provision in units, special classes or on an individual basis requires specialist teachers to be well-versed in the organization and practice of ordinary schools and to work in supportive and advisory roles with other teachers.

Teachers intending to specialize in particular aspects of special education will usually have developed their interest as a result of relevant teaching experience. When this is not the case, they should seek opportunities for observation or experience through which they can check that their interest is well-founded.

Preparation for a course of specialist study and training can take the form of participation in short courses and conferences, by appropriate reading or further study, for example, from the range of courses offered by the Open University. Journals and other publications by specialist subject teaching associations now more frequently refer to pupils with special educational needs. Associations particularly concerned with special educational needs are listed below.

Courses of specialist training for experienced teachers are listed in an annual DES list of long courses and are usually either one year full-time (with secondment from the LEA) or two years part-time. Some provide a general coverage of special educational needs and the curricular and teaching needs of children with difficulties in learning and adjustment. Some provide the specialist training for teaching hearing impaired or visually handicapped children and some provide for special attention to learning difficulties, emotional and behaviour difficulties or other specific needs. In practice, all courses should provide a broad knowledge of special needs and provisions as a base for whatever specialist skills are catered for.

Beyond this level, which obtains a qualification in special education, is the possibility of following a Master of Education course in special education. In some M.Ed. courses, special education may be studied as one of the required elements of the course which is useful for primary teachers or secondary subject teachers who are keen to extend their knowledge alongside their main field of interest. In a number of institutions, all the course work may bear upon special education in which case a first qualification or substantial experience in special education would normally be desirable or required.

For suitably qualified and experienced students, the opportunity of taking a higher degree (full-time or part-time) by research should be considered. There are many aspects of special education in which an individual researcher can make a valuable contribution to knowledge and practice.

Further reading

Association of Workers for Maladjusted Children (New Barns School, Church Lane, Toddington, Gloucestershire GL54 5DH) Journal: *Therapeutic Education*.

National Association for Remedial Education (2 Lichfield Road, Stafford ST17 4JX) Journal: *Remedial Education*.

National Council for Special Education (1 Wood Street, Stratford-upon-Avon, CV37 6JE) Journal: *Special Education: Forward Trends*.

Bibliography

AINSCOW, M. and TWEDDLE, D.A. (1979). *Preventing Classroom Failure: an objectives approach.* London: Wiley.

ALDRIDGE, H. (1982). 'The Gateway 2 course at Kingsway – Princeton College', *Educare*, 14, 23–25.

ANDERSON, E.M. (1976). 'Handwriting and spina bifida'. *Special Education*, 3, 2.

ANDERSON, E.M. and CLARKE, L. (1982). *Disability in Adolescence.* London: Methuen.

ANDERSON E. and TIZARD, J. (1983). 'Alternatives to work for severely handicapped people'. In: CLARKE, A.D.B. and TIZARD, B. *Child Development and Social Policy.* Leicester: British Psychological Society. Also in *The Education of the Handicapped Adolescent* (1983), OECD (obtainable HMSO).

ANDREWS, R.J., ELKINS, J., BERRY, P.B. and BURGE, J. (1979). *A Survey of Special Education in Australia.* St Lucia: University of Queensland.

ATKINSON, E.J. (1984). 'The adaptation of educationally subnormal leavers thirty years on', *Special Education*, 11, 4.

ATKINSON, E.J. and GAINS, C.W. (1985). *The New A–Z list of Reading Books.* Stafford: National Association for Remedial Education.

BAILEY, J. (1982). 'Special units in secondary schools', *Educational Review*, 34, 2.

BAILEY, T.J. (1982). 'Mathematics in the secondary school'. In: HINSON, M. and HUGHES, M. (Eds) *Planning Effective Progress.* Amersham: Hulton Educational.

BAILLIE, J. (1982). 'New initiatives – new hopes', *Special Education*, 9, 3.

BARNES, D. (1976). *From Communication to Curriculum.* Harmondsworth: Penguin.

BARNES, D., BRITTON, J. and ROSEN, H. (1971). *Language, the Learner and the School.* Harmondsworth: Penguin.

BELL, P. and KERRY, T. (1982). *Teaching Slow Learners.* London: Macmillan.

BLISHEN, E. (1955). *Roaring Boys: a schoolmaster's agony*. London: Thames and Hudson.

BOARDMAN, D. (Ed) (1982). *Geography for Slow Learners*. Sheffield: The Geographical Association.

BOOKBINDER, G.E. (1967). 'The preponderance of summer born children in ESN classes; which is responsible, age or length of schooling?', *Educational Research*, 9, 3.

BRADLEY, J. and HEGARTY, S. (1982). *Stretching the System*. London: Further Education Unit.

BRADLEY, T.B. (1983). 'Remediation of cognitive deficits: a critical appraisal of the Feuerstein model', *Journal of Mental Deficiency Research*, 27, 79–92.

BRENNAN, W.K. (1974). *Shaping the Education of Slow Learners*. London: Routledge and Kegan Paul.

BRENNAN, W.K. (1979). *Curricular Needs of Slow Learners* (Schools Council Working Paper 63). London: Evans/Methuen.

BRENNAN, W.K. (1982). *Special Education in Mainstream Schools*. Stratford-upon-Avon: National Council for Special Education.

BRENNER, N.W. (1967). 'Visuo-motor disability in school children', *British Medical Journal*, 4, 259–262.

BROWNE, G. (1979). *Continuing Education*: a programme for the less able in Colleges of Further Education. Manchester: Elfrida Rathbone Society.

BULLOCK REPORT. GREAT BRITAIN. DEPARTMENT OF EDUCATION AND SCIENCE (1975). *A Language for Life*. London: HMSO.

BURMAN, L., FARRELL, P., FEILER, A., MEFFERMAN, M. and MITTLER, M. (1983). 'Redesigning the school curriculum', *Special Education*, 10, 2.

BURT, C. (1937). *The Backward Child*. London: University of London Press.

BUSH, A. (1983). 'Can reading be improved by involving their parents?', *Remedial Education*, 18, 4.

BUSWELL, G.T. (1945). *Non-oral Reading: a study of its use in Chicago Schools*. Chicago: University of Chicago Press.

BUTTON, L. (1981). *Group Tutoring for the Form Teacher*. London: Hodder and Stoughton Educational.

CAMERON, R.J. (1981). 'Curriculum development. 1. clarifying and planning curriculum objectives', *Remedial Education*, 16, 4.

CAMERON, R.J. (Ed) (1982). *Working Together: Portage in the UK*. Windsor: NFER-NELSON.

CAWLEY, N. (1976). 'Social mathematics: remediation or stimulation?' *Remedial Education*, 11, 2.

CHAZAN, M. (1964). 'The incidence and nature of maladjustment among children in schools for the educationally subnormal', *British Journal of Educational Psychology*, 34, 3.

CHAZAN, M. (1967). 'The effects of remedial teaching in reading: a review of research', *Remedial Education*, 2, 1.

CHAZAN, M., LAING, A., BAILEY, M.S. and JONES, G. (1980). *Some of Our Children.* Shepton Mallet: Open Books.

CLARK, M.M. (1974). *Teaching Left Handed Children.* London: Hodder and Stoughton.

CLARK, M.M. (1979). *Reading Difficulties in Schools.* London: Heinemann Educational.

CLAY, M.M. (1972). *Reading: the Patterning of Complex Behaviour.* London: Heinemann Educational.

CLAY, M.M. (1979). *The Early Detection of Reading Difficulties.* London: Heinemann Educational.

CLUNIES-ROSS, L. and WIMHURST, S. (1983). *The Right Balance.* Windsor: NFER-NELSON.

COCKROFT REPORT. GREAT BRITAIN. DEPARTMENT OF EDUCATION AND SCIENCE (1982). *Mathematics Counts.* London: HMSO.

CORDTS, A.D. (1965). *Phonics for the Reading Teacher.* New York: Holt, Rinehart and Winston.

CORNWALL, K. and SPICER, J. (1982). 'The role of the educational psychologist in the discovery and assessment of children requiring special education'. Leicester: British Psychological Society. DECP Occasional publications, 6, 2.

COTTERELL, G.C. (1970). 'Teaching Procedures'. In: FRANKLIN, A.W. and NAIDOO, S. (Eds) *Assessment and Teaching of Dyslexic Children.* London: Invalid Children's Aid Association.

COWIE, E.E. (1979). *History and the Slow Learning Child.* London: The Historical Association.

DAVID, K. (1983). *Personal and Social Education in Schools.* London: Longmans for Schools Council.

DEAN, A. and HEGARTY, S. (1984). *Learning for Independence.* London: Further Education Unit.

DENVIR, B., STOLZ, C. and BROWN, M. (1982). *Low Attainers in Mathematics 5–16.* London: Methuen Educational.

DOUGHTY, P., PEARCE, J. and THORNTON, G. (1971). *Language in Use.* London: Edward Arnold.

DUNCAN, D. (1978). *Teaching Mathematics to Slow Learners.* London: Ward Lock.

DOWNING, J. (1969). 'ita and Slow Learners – a re-appraisal', *Educational Research,* 11, 3.

ENNEVER, L. (1972). *With Objectives in Mind:* Guide to Science 5–13. London: Macdonald Educational.

ERIKSON, E.H. (1965). *Childhood and Society.* London: Penguin.

FERGUSON, N. and ADAMS, M. (1982). 'Assessing the advantages of team teaching in remedial education', *Remedial Education,* 17, 1.

FERNALD, G. (1943). *Remedial Techniques in the Basic School Subjects.* New York: McGraw Hill.

FEUERSTEIN, R. (1980). *Instrumental Enrichment.* Baltimore: University Park Press.

FITZGERALD, A. (1984). 'The Mathematics in Employment project: its findings and implications', *Mathematics in School,* 12, 1 and 2.

FLEEMAN, A.M. (1984). 'From special to secondary school for children with moderate learning difficulties', *Special Education,* 11, 13.

FOGELMAN, K. (1976). *Britain's Sixteen Year Olds.* London: National Children's Bureau.

FRANCIS, J. and PHILLIPS-JOHNSON, S. (1984). 'A veritable Aladdin's Cave', *Remedial Education,* 19, 1.

FURTHER EDUCATION UNIT (1980). *Beyond Coping : some approaches to social education.* Further Education Curriculum Review and Development Unit.

FURTHER EDUCATION UNIT (1979; revised 1982). *A Basis for Choice.* London: FEU.

GARNETT, J. (1976). 'Special children in a comprehensive', *Special Education,* 3, 1.

GARNETT, J. (1983). 'Providing access to the mainstream curriculum in secondary schools'. In: BOOTH, T. and POTTS, P. (Eds) *Integrating Special Education.* Oxford: Blackwell.

GILLHAM, B. (1978). *Reconstructing Educational Psychology.* London: Croom Helm.

GILLHAM, B. (1981). *Problem Behaviour in the Secondary School.* London: Croom Helm.

GILLILAND, J. (1972). *Readability.* London: Hodder and Stoughton.

GLYNN, E. (1980). 'Parent child interaction in remedial reading at home'. In: CLARK, M.M. and GLYNN, E.C. (Eds) *Reading and Writing for the Child with Difficulties.* University of Birmingham: Educational Review, Occasional Publications No. 8.

GLYNN, E.C., THOMAS, J.D. and WOTHERSPIN. (1978). 'Applied psychology in the Mangere guidance unit', *Exceptional Child,* 25, 2.

GOLBY, M. and GULLIVER, J.R. (1979). 'Whose remedies, whose ills? A critical review of remedial education', *Journal of Curriculum Studies,* 11, 137–47.

GOLDSTEIN, H. and SEIGLE, D. (1958). *The Illinois Curriculum Guide.* Springfield, Illinois: Superintendant of Public Instruction.

GORDON, M. (1983). '"Because they are better than us!" Planning for failure in the secondary school', *Remedial Education,* 18, 4.

GREAT BRITAIN. BOARD OF EDUCATION (1937). *The Education of Backward Children.* London: HMSO.

GREAT BRITAIN. DEPARTMENT OF EDUCATION AND SCIENCE (1971). Education Survey No. 15: *Slow Learners in Secondary Schools.* London: HMSO.

GREAT BRITAIN. DEPARTMENT OF EDUCATION AND SCIENCE (1977). Curriculum 11–16: working papers by HM inspectorate. London: HMSO.

GREAT BRITAIN. DEPARTMENT OF EDUCATION AND SCIENCE (1978a). *Primary Education in England*. London: HMSO.

GREAT BRITAIN. DEPARTMENT OF EDUCATION AND SCIENCE (1978b). *Mixed Ability Work in Comprehensive Schools*. London: HMSO.

GREAT BRITAIN. DEPARTMENT OF EDUCATION AND SCIENCE (1979). *Aspects of Secondary Education in England*. London: HMSO.

GREAT BRITAIN. DEPARTMENT OF EDUCATION AND SCIENCE (1980). *A Framework for the Curriculum*. London: HMSO.

GREAT BRITAIN. DEPARTMENT OF EDUCATION AND SCIENCE (1981). *The School Curriculum*. London: HMSO.

GREAT BRITAIN. DEPARTMENT OF EDUCATION AND SCIENCE (1981). *Education Act 1981*. London: HMSO.

GREAT BRITAIN. DEPARTMENT OF EDUCATION AND SCIENCE (1983). *Circular 1/83. Assessments and Statements of Special Educational Needs*. London: HMSO.

GREAT BRITAIN. DEPARTMENT OF EDUCATION AND SCIENCE (1983). *Curriculum 11–16:* Towards a statement of entitlement. London: HMSO.

GREAT BRITAIN. SCOTTISH EDUCATION DEPARTMENT (1978). *The Education of Pupils with Learning Difficulties in Primary and Secondary Schools in Scotland*. Edinburgh: HMSO.

GREAT BRITAIN. SCOTTISH EDUCATION DEPARTMENT (1981). *The Education of Mildly Mentally Handicapped Pupils of Secondary School Age*. Edinburgh: HMSO.

GULLIFORD, R. and WIDLAKE, P. (1975). *Teaching Materials for Disadvantaged Pupils*. Schools Council Curriculum Bulletin 5. London: Evans/Methuen.

GUNSTONE, C., HOGG, J., SEBBA, J., WARNER, J. and ALMOND, S. (1982). *Classroom Provision and Organization for Integrated Pre-school Children*. Barkingside: Dr Barnardo's.

GURALNICK, M.J. (Ed) (1978). *Early Intervention and the Integration of Handicapped and Non-handicapped Children*. Baltimore: University Park Press.

HALLAM. R. (1982). 'History'. In HINSON, M. and HUGHES, M. (Eds) *Planning Effective Progress*. Amersham: Hulton Educational.

HALLIDAY, M.A.K. (1969). 'Relevant Models of Language', *Educational Review*, 22, 1.

HALLMARK, N. and DESSENT. T. (1982). 'A special education service centre', *Special Education*, 9, 1.

HAMMOND, D. (1967). 'Reading attainment in the primary schools of Brighton', *Educational Research*, 10, 1.

HARGREAVES, D.H. (1967). *Social Relations in a Secondary School*. London: Routledge and Kegan Paul.

HARROP, A. (1983). *Behaviour Modification in the Classroom*. London: Hodder and Stoughton.

HAWISHER, M.F. and CALHOUN, M.L. (1978). *The Resource Room*. Columbus, Ohio: Merrill.

HEGARTY, S. and POCKLINGTON, K. with LUCAS, D. (1981). *Educating Pupils with Special Needs in the Ordinary School*. Windsor: NFER-NELSON.

HEGARTY, S. and POCKLINGTON, K. with LUCAS, D. (1982). *Integration in Action*. Windsor: NFER-NELSON.

HEWISON, J. (1982). 'Parental involvement in the teaching of reading', *Remedial Education*, 17, 4.

HEWITT, F. (1964). 'A hierarchy of educational tasks for children with learning disorders', *Exceptional Children*, 31, 207–214.

HILDRETH, G.H. (1955). *Teaching Spelling*. New York: Holt, Rinehart and Winston.

HINSON, M. and HUGHES, M. (1982). *Planning Effective Progress*. Amersham: Hulton/National Association for Remedial Education.

HUTCHINSON, D. (1982). *Work Preparation for the Handicapped*, London: Croom Helm.

HUTCHINSON, D. and CLEGG, N. (1975). 'Orientated towards work', *Special Education*, 2, 1.

INGRAM, A.J. (1958). 'Elementary education in England during the period of payment by results.' Unpublished dissertation: University of Birmingham.

JERROLD, M.A. and FOX, R. (1968). 'Pre-jobs for the boys', *Special Education*, 57, 2.

JOHNSON, D.J. and MYKLEBUST, H.R. (1967). *Learning Disabilities*. New York: Grune and Stratton.

JOHNSON, T.D. (1973). *Reading: Teaching and Learning*. London: Macmillan.

JONES, E. and BERRICK, S. (1980). 'Adopting a resourceful approach', *Special Education*, 7, 1.

JONES, N. (1971). 'The Brislington Project in Bristol', *Special Education*, 60, 2.

JONES, N. (1973). 'Special adjustment units in comprehensive schools', *Therapeutic Education*, 1, 2.

KELLMER PRINGLE, M.L. (1975). *The Needs of Children*. London: Hutchinson.

KELLMER PRINGLE, M.L., BUTLER, N.R. and DAVIE, R. (1966). *11,000 Seven Year Olds*. London: Longmans.

KERSHAW, I.L. (1978). 'Science 14–16'. In: HINSON, M. (Ed) *Encouraging Results*. London: Macdonald Educational.

KERRY, T. and SANDS, M. (Eds) (1982). *Mixed Ability Teaching*. London: Macmillan Educational.

LABON, D. (1973). 'Helping maladjusted children in primary schools', *Therapeutic Education*.

LASLETT, R.B. (1982). *Maladjusted Children in the Ordinary School*. Stratford-upon-Avon: National Council for Special Education.

LASLETT, R.B. and SMITH, C. (1984). *Effective Classroom Management.* London: Croom Helm.

LAWRENCE, D. (1971). 'Counselling of retarded readers by non-professionals', *Educational Research,* 15, 2.

LEWIS, G. (1984). 'A supportive role at secondary level', *Remedial Education,* 19, 1.

LOWDEN, G. (1984). 'Integrating slow learners in Wales', *Special Education,* 11, 4.

LUNZER, E. and GARDNER, K. (Eds) (1979). *The Effective Use of Reading.* London: Heinemann.

LUNZER, E. and GARDNER, K. (1982). *Learning from the Written Word.* Edinburgh: Oliver and Boyd.

MACDAID, M.M. (1982). 'Young people with learning difficulties in Work Introduction Courses', *Educational Review,* 34, 2.

MCIVER, V. (Ed) (1982). *Teaching History to Slow Learning Children in Secondary Schools.* Belfast: Stranmillis College.

MACKAY, D., THOMPSON, B. and SCHAUB, P. (1970). *Breakthrough to Literacy.* London: Longmans.

MCPHAIL, P. (1972). *Moral Education Curriculum Project.* Harlow: Longmans.

MARLAND, M. (1975). *The Craft of the Classroom – a survival guide.* London: Heinemann.

MARLAND, M. (1977). *Language Across the Curriculum.* London: Heinemann Educational.

MARRA, M.E. (1981). 'The incidence and nature of secondary handicaps among children in day ESN schools', *Remedial Education,* 16, 2.

MASSIE, B. (1982). 'Significant living without work', *Special Education,* 9, 3.

MILES, T.R. and E. (1983). *Help for Dyslexic Children.* London: Methuen.

MINISTRY OF EDUCATION (1946). *Special Education Treatment.* London: HMSO.

MINISTRY OF EDUCATION (1950). *Reading Ability.* London: HMSO.

MITTLER, P. (1979). *People Not Patients.* London: Methuen.

MOORE, N. (1957). 'A survey of the use of arithmetic in the daily life of adults'. Unpublished dissertation: University of Birmingham.

MORRIS, M. (1966). *Standards and Progress in Reading.* Windsor: NFER.

MOSES, D. (1982). 'Special educational needs: relationship between teacher assessment, test scores and classroom behaviour', *British Educational Research Journal,* 8, 2.

MUNCEY, J. and AINSCOW, M. (1983). 'Launching SNAP in Coventry', *Special Education,* 10, 3.

MUNCEY, J. and WILLIAMS, H. (1981). 'Daily evaluation in the classroom', *Special Education,* 8, 3.

PEEL, E.A. (Ed))1972). 'The Quality of Understanding in Secondary School Subjects', *Educational Review,* 24, 3.

PERERA, K. (1981). 'Some language problems in school learning'. In: MERCER, N. *Language in School and Community*. London: Edward Arnold.

PETERS, M.L. (1979). 'Spelling: generalization not rules', *Special Education*, 6, 1.

PETERSON, D. (1972). *Functional Mathematics for Slow Learners*. Ohio: Charles E. Merrill.

PHILLIPS, C.J. (1982). 'Specific learning difficulties: some reflections of a practical psychologist', *Educational Review*, 34, 2.

PINFIELD, B. (1982). 'Mathematics for primary children with learning difficulties'. In: HINSON, M. and HUGHES, M. (Eds) *Planning Effective Progress*. Amersham: Hulton.

PLOWDEN REPORT. GREAT BRITAIN. DEPARTMENT OF EDUCATION AND SCIENCE (1967). *Children and their Primary Schools*. London: HMSO.

POCKLINGTON, K. (1980). 'Integration – a lesson from America', *Special Education*, 7, 3.

POTEET, J.A. (1973). *Behaviour Modification: a practical guide*. London: Hodder and Stoughton.

PUGH, G. (Ed) (1981). *Parents as Partners*. London: National Children's Bureau.

RAYBOULD, E. and SOLITY, J. (1972). 'Teaching with precision', *Special Education*, 9, 2.

REDL, F. and WINEMAN, D. (1952). *Controls from Within*. New York: Free Press.

REID, J.F. (1966). 'Learning to think about reading', *Educational Research*, 9, 1.

REID, J.F. (1972). *Reading: Problems and Practices*. London: Ward Lock.

REID, M., CLUNIES-ROSS, L., GOACHER, B. and VILE, C. (1981). *Mixed Ability Teaching: problems and possibilities*. Windsor: NFER-NELSON.

RODWAY, A. (Ed) (1981). *Day Units for Children with Emotional and Behavioural Difficulties*. Association for Workers with Maladjusted Children.

RUTTER, M., COX, A., TUPLING, C., BERGER, M. and YULE, W. (1975). 'Attainment and adjustment in two geographical areas. 1. The prevalence of psychiatric disorder', *British Journal of Psychiatry*, 126, 493–509.

RUTTER, M., MAUGHAN, B., MORTIMORE, P. and OUSTON, J. (1979). *Fifteen Thousand Hours*, London: Open Books.

RUTTER, M., TIZARD, J. and WHITMORE, K. (1970). *Education, Health and Behaviour*. London: Longmans.

SAKAMOTO, T. (1978). 'Beginning reading in Japan'. In: THACKERAY, D. (Ed) *Growth in Reading*. London: Ward Lock Educational.

SAMPSON, O. (1975). *Remedial Education*. London: Routledge and Kegan Paul.

SANDS, M. (1982). 'Teaching Methods: myth and reality'. In: SANDS, M. and KERRY, T. *Mixed Ability Teaching*. London: Croom Helm.

SAYER, J. (1983a). 'Assessment for all, statements for none', *Special Education.* 10, 4.

SAYER, J. (1983b). 'A comprehensive school for all'. In: BOOTH, A. and POTTS, P. (Eds) *Integrating Special Education,* Oxford: Blackwell.

SCHONELL, F.J. (1942). *Backwardness in the Basic Subjects.* Edinburgh: Oliver and Boyd.

SCOTTISH COUNCIL FOR RESEARCH IN EDUCATION (1961). *Studies in Spelling.* London: University of London Press.

SEWELL, B. (1980). *The Mathematical Needs of Adults in Daily Life.* London: Advisory Council for Adult and Continuing Education.

SHEARER, E. (1977). 'A survey of ESN(m) children in Cheshire', *Special Education,* 4, 2.

SKEMP, R.R. (1971). *The Psychology of Learning Mathematics.* Harmondsworth: Penguin.

SOUTHGATE, V., ARNOLD, H. and JOHNSON, S. (1981). *Extending Beginning Reading.* London: Heinemann Educational.

TATE, N. (1979). 'Can we re-create the past?' *Special Education,* 6, 3.

TAVERNER, D.T. (1980). *Developing a Reading Programme.* London: Ward Lock.

TAYLOR, R. (Ed) (1981). *Ways and Means 2.* Basingstoke: Macmillan.

THOMPSON, G.E. (1962). 'What arithmetic shall we teach educationally subnormal children?' *Special Education,* 51.

TIZARD REPORT. GREAT BRITAIN. DEPARTMENT OF EDUCATION AND SCIENCE. SECRETARY OF STATE'S ADVISORY COMMITTEE (1972). *Children with Specific Reading Difficulties.* London: HMSO.

TIZARD, J., SCHOFIELD, W.N. and HEWISON, J. (1982). 'Collaboration between teachers and parents in assisting children's reading', *British Journal of Educational Psychology,* 52, 1–15.

TIZARD, J. and ANDERSON, E. (1983). 'The education of the handicapped adolescent; alternatives to work for severely handicapped people'. In: CLARKE, A.D.B. and TIZARD, B. (Eds) *Child Development and Social Policy.* Leicester: British Psychological Society.

TOMLINSON, S. (1982). *A Sociology of Special Education.* London: Routledge and Kegan Paul.

TOPPING, K. and MCKNIGHT, G. (1984). 'Paired reading – and parent power', *Special Education,* 11, 3.

TOUGH, J. (1977). *Talking and Learning: a guide to fostering communication skills in nursery and infant schools.* London: Ward Lock.

TUCKEY, L., PARFIT, J. and TUCKEY, R. (1973). *Handicapped School Leavers: their Further Education and Training.* Slough: National Foundation for Educational Research.

VINCENT, D., GREEN, L., FRANCIS, J. and POWNEY, J. (1983). *A Review of Reading Tests.* Windsor: NFER-NELSON.

WALKER, C. (1974). *Reading Development and Extension.* London: Ward Lock.

WARNOCK, M. (1978). *Special Educational Needs*. London: HMSO.

WARNOCK REPORT. GREAT BRITAIN. DEPARTMENT OF EDUCATION AND SCIENCE (1978). *Special Educational Needs*. London: HMSO.

WEBB, L. (1967). *Children with Special Needs in the Infant School*. London: Colin Smyth.

WEDGE, P. and PROSSER, H. (1973). *Born to Fail?* Arrow Books/NCB.

WELLER, K. and CRAFT, A. (1983). *Making Up Our Minds*. London: Schools Council.

WHITEHEAD, F., CAPEY, F.C. and MADDREN, W. (1974). *Children's Reading Interests*. London: Evans/Methuen.

WIEDERHOLT, J.L., HAMMILL, D. and BROWN, V. (1975). *The Resource Teacher*. Boston: Allyn and Bacon.

WILLIAMS, M. (1982). 'Geography' In: HINSON, M. and HUGHES, M. *Planning Effective Progress*. Amersham: Hulton Educational.

WILLIAMS, P. (1964). 'Date of birth, backwardness and educational organization', *British Journal of Educational Psychology*, 34.

WILLIAMS, P. and GRUBER, E. (1967). *Response to Special Schooling*. London: Longmans.

WILLIAMS, T. and WILLIAMS, N. (1980). *Personal and Social Development in the School Curriculum*. London: Schools Council.

WILSON, G.M. (1919). *A Survey of Social and Business Usage of Arithmetic*. Teachers' College Contributions to Education, no. 100. New York: Columbia Teachers' College.

WILSON, M. (1981). *The Curriculum in Special Schools*. London: Schools Council.

WILTON, V.M.E. (1975). 'A mother helper scheme in the infant school', *Educational Research*, 18, 1.

WOLFENDALE, S. and BRYANS, T. (1980). *Identification of Learning Difficulties*. Stafford: National Association for Remedial Education.

WRAGG, E.C. (1978). 'Death by a thousand worksheets', *Times Educational Supplement*, no. 3305, 3, p. 20.

YOUNG, P. and TYRE, C. (1983). *Dyslexia or Illiteracy?* Milton Keynes: Open University Press.

YULE, W. (1973). 'Differential prognosis of reading backwardness and specific reading retardation', *British Journal of Educational Psychology*, 43, 3.

Index